GUIDE COLLOMB

3. Picos de Europa
Northern Spain

D1512781

Peña Santa de Castilla.   Drawing by Schrader from a photo by Saint-Saud, 1893

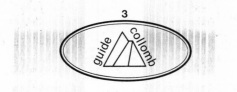

PICOS DE EUROPA
NORTHERN SPAIN

ROBIN G. COLLOMB

West Col

PICOS DE EUROPA
Northern Spain

First published 1983 by
West Col Productions
Goring   Reading   Berks. RG8 9AA

SBN 906227 23 2

Printed in England by Swindon Press Ltd
Swindon   Wilts.

Contents

Illustrations

Uncredited drawings and diagrams by Stephanie Collomb

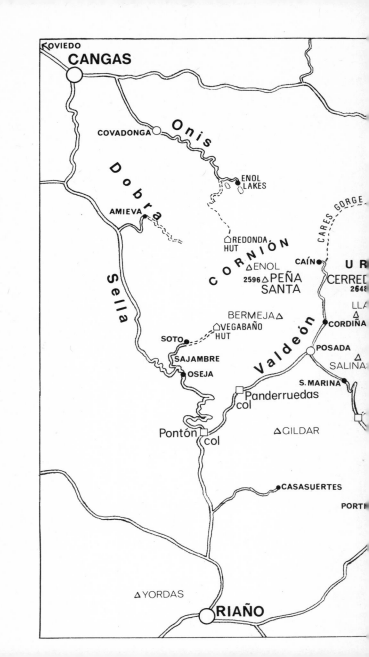

PICOS DE EUROPA

0 1 2 3 4 5   10 km

SHORT GLOSSARY

Aguja	aiguille, needle (Ag.)
Alto	prominent mountain top
Canal	steep gully or gorge
Collada, Collado	col, pass (Ca., Co.)
Horca, Horcada, Horcadina	narrow pass (Ha.)
Horreo	barn
Hoyo	deep circular depression, sink hole
Invernales	winter quarters
Jito	upright splinter of rock used as waymark
Jou	see Hoyo
Llambrias	smooth slabby rock
Lloroza	rainy (hollow)
Majada	area of stone huts and sheepfolds
Mirador	viewpoint
Neverón	snowslopes
Peña	sharp rock peak (P.)
Posada	inn
Pico	peak (P.)
Puerto	gate – pass
Risco	isolated crag, usually a secondary pinnacled summit
Tiro	chamois hide, applied to summits, passes, large terraces, etc. (To.)
Torre	tower-like summit (Te.)
Vega	small plateau, depression/plain with greenery
Vernales	summer quarters
Venta	lodging house

Introductory

THE PICOS DE EUROPA form the apex of the Cantabrian Mountains (Cordillera Cantábrica) and pursue a course parallel to the northern seaboard of Spain. Outside the Sierra Nevada in Granada to the far south, and chains of the Pyrenees shared along the frontier with France, these summits have no equal in height throughout the Iberian peninsula and are unrivalled for splendid rock scenery. The massif rises about 25 km. inland from the Costa Verde (Green Coast) with its centre about 90 km. WSW of Santander port. Altogether the inner area measures 35 km. E-W and 15km. N-S; roadways into and round the massif incur journeys of threefold disance. As a rectangular zone it divides into three distinct groups, called simply East, Central and West. The western part is a national park, created in 1918, and the habitat of thousands of free-roaming chamois (rebecos); **the central group** contains the dominant peaks and is therefore the most visited; the eastern group is scarred by mining operations (zinc and manganese) and receives undeservedly little attention. Excluding the Pyrenees the Picos massif is now the most frequented Spanish mountain area in summer by foreign visitors. Among the many natural regions of outstanding beauty and interest in Spain only the Picos de Europa, Andorra and Montserrat are awarded the highest accolade of three stars in the Michelin rating system; selected areas of the Pyrenees, Sierra Nevada and Sierra de Gredos rate only two stars, although a few "sights" in these regions are given three as places of unusual scenic merit. The Michelin guide to Spain (in English) is recommended for exploring the coastal and hinterland districts round the Picos de Europa, especially for visiting numerous cave dwellings which contain prehistoric paintings and engravings, those at Altamira being the earliest discovery of Palaeolithic art in Europe.

The boundaries of three provinces meet at the summit of Pico Tesorero in the central group; Oviedo on the N side, León to the W, and Santander to the E. Recently they have joined forces as a homogeneous Cantábrica Region for the purpose of waging a low-key political campaign against central government for autonomy and self rule in domestic matters, following the partial breakaway achieved by the neighbouring Basque provinces. Historically this region is embraced by the older and larger principality of Asturias, where the original kingdom of Spain was established. It is famous for its militant coal mining communities whose ancestors preserved Christianity on the northern slopes of the Cantabrian Mountains by resisting Moslem invaders occupying the central plains. Asturian autonomy is synonymous with Cantabrian. The decisive battle, turning the tide against the Moorish forces and eventually causing them to be driven out of Spain, took place at Covadonga in 722 under the leadership of Pelayo, a tribal chief who claimed descent from the dynasty of Visigothic monarchs. The "Reconquista" of Spain thus began. In 1934 and 1936-7 in a prelude to the Spanish Civil War the Asturian miners rose up and fought government forces in battles at Oviedo which was held by the insurgents for some time.

Despite widespread mining activities the chief occupations for the Cantabrian peoples are agriculture, deep sea fishing and whaling. The most likely origin of the otherwise obscure name for the prominent horned peaks of this massif is the first - and last - sight of mainland Spain and Europe glimpsed by fishermen returning home across the Bay of Biscay from long voyages to the northern seas.

The jagged peaks of the Picos can be regarded as the most compact exposure of scenic mountain limestone in Western Europe. The Dolomites of Italy are scattered over a wider area and are divided into many groups by a network of broad valleys. The Northern Limestone ranges of Austria are distinctly carved from escarpment formations, or from a single ridge –

like the Kaisergebirge. Other groups with a passing likeness to the Picos are smaller both in extent and sometimes altitude. The Julian Alps of Slovenia and Italy compare more closely, having a look alike zone of crowded pinnacles in the Italian part but more extensive vegetation covering essentially larger and dispersed summit areas in Slovenia.

The Picos remain unique for revealing a large mountain block carved by narrow defiles (desfiladeros, gargantas, etc.) whose sheer walls rise in places for 1000m. These impressive chasms relent at a variable altitude, roughly between 1200 and 1600m. Above that are scanty pastures for grazing sheep, goats and sometimes cows (vegas = small plateaus, comparable with the term alp or alm but rarely as valuable or prized as the latter), then cirques of scree (graveras), terraces of rock and finally sharp peaks whose continuously steep rockfaces measure 300-500m. in height. Walls in the upper mountain zone of 600m. are exceptional while a few of 800m. or more might be found.

Taking the region as a whole fretwork crests unfold a multitude of peaks and weave in all directions. From many viewpoints their prickly outlines merge into a confusing array of cockscombs. Deep gorges (canals) and huge circular hollows called hoyos (jous in the local dialect), some exceeding one km. in diameter, divide this maze of ridges. The crater-like floors of these hoyos, as much as 150m. deep and filled with white rock corrugated by thousands of crevices, convey to the onlooker a lunar landscape likewise devoid of water. Depressions in ridges and between evident summits often look alike so that it is difficult to distinguish, except at close quarters, between an easy col (collado, horcada) and a ridge gap for rock climbers. Some of the most important ridge crossings have one especially delicate flank.

This barren landscape posed a topographical puzzle of considerable magnitude to the first explorers which is still not wholly solved to judge by the mapping available to date. As an area once celebrated for its complexity and lack of information for making correct approaches and crossings of its rugged terrain, the pleasures of discovery and unravelling the nature of mistakes in route finding can still be enjoyed, and can even prove quite formidable in poor visability for the first-time visitor. Writing in 1872 John Ormsby concluded: "The interior of the massif is something in form like a very dilapidated honeycomb; a labyrinth of crater-like basins separated by walls bristling with aiguilles, all bearing the strongest possible family likeness one to the other ... looking at the Picos de Europa from any elevation it would appear about as hopeless to go in search of the highest peak as it would to try to determine which is absolutely the tallest spine on the back of a hedgehog."

A popular belief about the Picos states that its major peaks are fairly easy of access on their N sides, while presenting difficulties and big cliffs on the S - the reverse of most alpine situations. This holds true about half the time, with an extreme reversal instanced by the famous Naranjo peak. In the context of mountain walking and touring, first class summits are always significant diversions from cross-country routes furnished with discernible paths. The only good paths are those constructed for access to mine workings, old and new, and more recently waterworks; the western section of the region has some paths much improved by the national park authority. Paths otherwise can be tricky to follow over the rough terrain where cairns and waymarks are placed at long intervals. It is all too easy to wander into a huge hoyo when an unlikely-looking but feasible line could be taken round its rocky walls.

The limestone (Karst) of the Picos is exceptionally compact, sound and smooth; yet it has a superbly rough surface, weathered by water action, as to give excellent friction underfoot. It excels in this feature as a quality unmatched by any limestone region in the Alps. This characteristic slabby rock is called locally "llambrias" after the name of the second highest point in the region. A consequence of so much bare rock devoid of

14

vegetation are large areas of scree and shin-barking boulder fields tanta-
mount to the most dispicable walking terrain imaginable. There are "secret"
ways of avoiding a lot of this ground but only intimate knowledge will
gradually disclose these to the visitor.

Rainfall and snowmelt run below ground immediately, so that no running
water can be found generally above 1600m. A few large pools collect in
the smaller hoyos with earthy beds. Water reappears lower down as lively
streams in the main valleys which by contrast are filled with luxuriant
vegetation. Many of these streams are **badly polluted, especially** near
villages. Springs (fuentes) can be found in the upper zones where sub-
terranean water bubbles to the surface in a pan-size opening; these springs
are marked on several current maps (if not too accurately) and it is useful
to learn their exact whereabouts. Other than these, old snow patches are
the only source for collecting water. In practice parties staying in one
locality where water is scarce frequently carry in a water supply for their
needs.

Proximity to the ocean and the humid temperate climate of the Costa
Verde ensure that the Picos are veiled by damp weather for much of the
year. The immediate hinterland to the S is notably drier. In spring and
early summer rainfall tends to be plentiful; cloud cover is frequent except
during the evening. A fine on-shore rain from the Atlantic is known
locally as orbayu. July and August have a combined average rainfall of
2 in. In this period dense mist attends early morning, followed after
short clear periods by a cloud blanket until early evening. There might
be days without rain when a luminous fog smothers the shining white limestone wilderness and defeats all the skill an experienced party can muster
to find the way. The best continuously clear spell is recorded as the last
week of August and the first two of September - often prolonged well into
this month. Then an immense sea of cloud fills the encroaching valleys to
a height of 1500m., while the summit areas stand out bright and clear above

it all day long. Violent winds can be experienced in all weather conditions between May and September. At other times the region is very wet with considerable snowfall in winter and early spring. The average annual precipitation compares with the Scottish Highlands, 60 in. or more. Winter visits to the Picos are for making ascents in this season of summer routes in the alpine sense, or for rather tough cross-country skiing; both have only a small following at present. The ascent of normal routes on these mountains in typical winter conditions can be quite hazardous due to knife edges of soft snow and unconsolidated cornices. Sound local judgement is necessary to ascertain good conditions for winter climbing in the region.

Piste skiing and winter sports, developed among gentler summits elsewhere in the Cantabrian chain, have no great future in the Picos. A skitow has been erected behind the Fuente Dé cableway and similar small projects are being tried elsewhere. New developments on the southern outer edges of the region seem likely to gain some popularity, especially at Riaño. Further E, the Alto Campóo group near Reinosa is the main skiing area for Santander and Bilbao residents.

Most of the winter snowfall disperses after July; before that, in May and June, long snow tongues and icy headslopes require the use of axe and crampons. Permanent and normally icy snowbands and inlets last throughout the season in numerous well known places. These invariably co-incide with walking and scrambling routes to principal peaks. In the writer's experience these places always call for an axe, and sometimes crampons, to ensure complete safety, although alternative routes may be available to avoid them. Conspicuous examples are found on both Peña Santa peaks and the Llambrión. The Spanish are noted for laxity in emphasising that parties should equip themselves with snow/ice equipment up to mid-summer and even later for several popular objectives.

One assumes that the harshness of this mountain desert accounts for the paucity of wildlife. Bears and wolves were masters of the domain 100 years ago but they have been progressively hunted and slaughtered into extinction. Small animals of the rodent family, like marmots and species of mice so common in the Alps, are entirely absent from human gaze. Chamois can be seen almost anywhere, singly or moving in small herds; they display unusual timidity and willingness to approach man closely, due no doubt in part to a total ban on hunting throughout the year. Amazing agility and ability to scale apparently smooth and sheer rockfaces are no less evident here than demonstrations of acrobatic feats given by the same family in the Alps and elsewhere. Reptiles are also scarce save for a variety of lizard. More numerous are salamanders (a newt), beautifully striped in black and gold, living in holes containing water trapped below ground at elevations of about 1500-2000m. They emerge in great numbers, often along rocky footpaths, in misty weather and during or just after heavy rain showers. Armies of these pleasant colourful creatures occupy the ground immediately above the Vega Redonda hut in the western Picos. Also in this district wild horses roam the pastures round the Enol/Ercina lakes.

Another common sight are great birds aloft. The largest golden eagles and ptarmigan found in any European mountains haunt the tall crags and cannot be missed on a fine day. Trout is plentiful in the main river valleys and those draining to the sea have salmon in spring and early summer.

The flora is a disappointment for the botanist. So little soil can rest in suitable crannies in this wilderness that even hardy Alpine flowers have a struggle to establish themselves and survive. Common alpine species grow in small pockets throughout the area but are diminished at the rate they might be discovered by herds of itinerant chamois. Gentians flourish abundantly in the Andara area of the massif.

Communications in the Picos consist of a good but narrow string of tarmac roads traversing all the valleys surrounding the triple massif. The outer ring, say from Panes back to Panes, amounts to 202 km., crosses two major passes (puertos) and other minor ones, and could hardly be accomplished in a day by public transport. Irregular bus services ply these roads. Branching from this encircling system are similar roads in side valleys that penetrate towards the base of the massif; these roads end in parking areas or jeep tracks (pistas); all the important ones have an infrequent bus service. The coastal railway after (W of) Santander is poor and uncomfortable, and visitors relying on public transport should use the somewhat more satisfactory bus services from this seaport. With roadheads terminating below huge rock walls supporting the massif - particularly the two chief points of entry at Fuente Dé and Puente Poncebos, no views of the interior are granted to those who remain at the bottom. However the regional tourist authority has made some effort to indicate good viewpoints (miradores) in the landscape by erecting large signboards at points elsewhere along the Picos roadway system. The most splendid of these, given clear conditions, is the Mirador de Llesba turn-off at the top of the Puerto de San Glorio, from where a magnificent panorama of the entire massif is revealed. Altogether, visitors with cars, whatever the nature of their journey, enjoy a considerable advantage over those without, especially when time is important.

Transport from Britain and car hire, accommodation, hotels, inns, huts and camping, restaurants and meals, foodstuffs and shopping, are described in the next section of the guide. In 1980 costs in this part of Spain corresponded closely with those of a modest approach to British mountain areas; certainly cheaper than most areas of the Alps notwithstanding a steep annual rate of inflation in Spain. Motor vehicle running costs (petrol, etc.) are more expensive than Britain (plus 25%).

PHYSICAL RELIEF AND TOPOGRAPHY

The two outer wings, east and west, of the region are roughly equal in area and balance in symmetrical fashion the larger oval central zone. The eastern wing in local terminology is the Macizo Oriental; its zonal name

De Andara identifies the northern facet where mining has been carried out. The eastern edge of this wing is clearly defined by the spectacular Hermida gorge, allowing the road from Panes to enter from the N along the snaking course of the Rio Deva to reach Potes. All this and the upper basin drained by the Deva is properly the Liébana valley. Potes is one of the three chief tourist resorts in the area and possibly the most agreeable.

The eastern wing is divided from the central by the Rio Duje. A broad upland saddle, Puertos de Aliva, at the top of the latter then gives birth to the Rio Nevandi which descends briefly in a valley S to Espinama where it enters the Deva. The notable summits of the eastern group are confined to a single twisting ridge: Morra (or Tabla) de Lechugales (2441m.), Picos del Jierro (2438m.), Pico del Evangelista (2426m.) and Pico Cortés (2370m.).

The tableland at the top of the Duje and Nevandi valleys contrasts vividly with the tremendous rock gorge that cuts off the W side of the central massif. The Rio Cares flows generally N from a point to the S of the Picos and so divides the central and western zones. At first it runs in a verdant and ever-deepening valley, with a broad bed and steep flanks. The walls eventually close to a mere cleft before expanding temporarily at a junction with the lateral Pasada valley. Here the hamlet of Caín (513m., road terminus from Posada de Valdeón), the most remote habitation in the Picos, is found among terraced fields. Below this point the river descends through the fabulous Garganta del Cares with its hair-raising catwalk trail, tunnels and flimsy bridges for 12 km. to Poncebos. The Macizo Central, or De Urrieles after pastoral features in the vicinity, has a focal point in the narrow saddle of the Rojos col, from where complicated ridges spread out in all directions. One to the NW carries the Torre Cerredo (2648m.), culminating point of the Picos de Europa. Another jagged crest to the W builds up to the Llambrión (2642m.). To the SE the largest object sighted is the mountain walker's viewpoint par excellence of the Peña Vieja (2613m.). While not by 20 summits the highest point in the NE segment of ridges, the fang-like tooth of the Naranjo de Bulnes (2519m.) - Picu de Urriellu to the natives and simply El Picu to climbers - dominates a forest of towers and pinnacles. For easy or hard ascents there are at least 40 worthwhile summits in the central massif. Rumour has it that there are over 300 first class rock climbs; however a keen eye for a good line could spot as many new ones again in a week but in doing so would not have the time to climb even one of them.

The western wing of the Picos differs from the other two in having a declining slope to the NW, down to the Enol lakes where lush grasslands resemble a conventional alpine scene. Disposed on two sides of this slope an elbow of peaks conforms to the intricate pattern associated with the rest of the region; it sprouts several knotty offshoots, not least in importance the great Peña Santa de Castilla (2596m.), an exceptional rock edifice regarded by many students of the area as the finest summit in all the Picos. It cannot be seen from the Enol tourist balconies, being hidden by another prominent summit on the skyline of domes and turrets; the popular imitator Peña Santa de Enol (2478m.) is more correctly called Torre de Santa Maria de Enol, though abbreviated on several maps to Te. Santa de Enol. The outer western edge of this area is delineated by the river valley of the Sella, running partly through vegetated gorges (beyos) from Cangas de Onis and afterwards over the Puerto del Pontón to Riaño further S. All mapping is most at fault in depicting the precise layout of peaks and passes crowded into the space between the two Peña Santas. The deceptive outward appearance of idyllic picturesque trekking country confronting the visitor who enters the Macizo Occidental from the Enol lakes belies the explanation of its domestic name Picos de Cornión; the last translates as the true "Horned Peaks" of the region, as arduous to approach as any if tried from the Rio Cares on the SE side of the group. Other summits of great interest include the Torre de Enmedio (2465m.), Torres del Torco (2450m.), Torres de Cebolleda (2438m.), La Torrezuela

(2302m.) and a host of less elevated spires. There are particularly worthwhile panoramic excursions and circular tours in this group for mountain walkers.

The Picos de Europa jut N of the main backbone of the Cantabrian Mountains. The San Glorio pass (1609m.) links them to the parent chain in a section called the Sierra de Alba or Alto Carrión - once thought to contain the highest summits of the system. It offers wild and remote walking country with considerable rock climbing potential of a character quite different from the Picos (predominantly conglomerates with some granite and limestone), and includes the Peña Prieta (2536m.), Curavacas (2520m.) and Espigüete (2450m.).

A wooded hogsback, the Sierra de Cuera (Turbina, 1315m.), separates the Picos from the Bay of Biscay shore between Ribadesella and Unquera. Mid distance between these two small towns the lobster fishing port of Llanes offers an attractive quiet seaside resort and haven from the rigours of the mountains; good campsite with services 5 km. to W near beach.

Massifs of the Cantabrian chain flanking the Picos to the E and W are: Alto Campóo or Sierra de Peña Labra, a highly developed skiing area with several lifts, appropriate hotel facilities and a road to an upper carpark area at nearly 2100m. The main summits are Cuchillón (2222m.) and Tres Mares (2175m.). A secondary massif comes between the Campóo area and the Liébana/Potes valley, culminating in the sugarloaf Peña Sagra (2046m.); it ranks as a first class outing on the opposite (E) side of the valley, where the W side is enclosed by the eastern (Andara) massif of the Picos.

On the SW side of the Picos, and reached from Riaño, rise the pointed peaks of the Pelayo group; Pico Yordas (1963m.) and Peñas Pintas (1983m.). Adjoining them is the well known nature reserve of Mampodre (2190m.).

o   o   o

La Hermida, at entrance to gorge. Contemporary print c. 1894

The discovery of zinc ores in the Picos encouraged the earliest forays into the upper rock wilderness, though summits were rarely visited. Local hunters wandered up secondary peaks, and a few major ones, in search of game. These men got themselves a reputation for bad memories; when they came into employment as guides for surveyors and tourists they often lost the way and could not find a previously recognised route to the summit.

Commercial exploitation aside, the pursuit of scientific knowledge and natural history attracted the first outsiders. In this context the Picos were discovered by D. Casiano de Prado (1797-1866), a Spanish mining engineer with interests in a number of exploratory fields. Two of his frequent companions were the French geologists MM. de Verneuil and de Lorière who thus establish from an early date a French connection with the region which later grew into the driving force behind exploration.

Casiano first saw the Picos in 1845. He attempted to penetrate the massif in 1851 but was defeated by bad weather. With his two French friends he came to Riaño in 1853 and entered the Valdeón basin from Portilla de la Reina to make what they believed was the first ascent of the Te. de Salinas (2446m.), a favoured viewpoint today. They thought that the Salinas ridge would culminate in the highest peaks of the region and were surprised to see a jigsaw of neighbouring ridges all clearly higher. After returning to the valley the inhabitants of Caín informed them that the Salinas had been climbed before by hunters, while a mountain called Te. del Llambrión was the ultimate point. An abortive attempt in 1855 caused Casiano to return with renewed determination in 1856 for the sole purpose of finding and climbing the Llambrión. Joined by an engineering friend Joaquim Boguerin he enlisted the help of five Valdeón hunters who led them across the Colladina de las Nieves into the Jou Oscuro, then over the Horcada Verde and round the hoyos and spurs under the NE side of the Tiro Llago-Torre Blanca chain into the saddle of the Collada Blanca.

23

From here they crossed the Llambrión glacier to reach the NE ridge of the mountain which rises gradually to the top. Casiano's description of the ascent is brief and vague and the route details have been deduced by historians. It corresponds to the easiest way today from the Verónica biv. hut. At the summit he did not fail to observe that another peak in plain view was "probably higher".

Casiano was content with this conquest and some 15 years elapsed before more news of exploration drifted to the outside world. An English barrister John Ormsby (1827-1895), who had joined the Alpine Club in the first year of its existence, had taken upon himself a quixotic exploration of Spanish mountains. When he reached the Picos he was astonished by what he saw and knew straightaway that "to anyone with an indomitable passion for scrambling, the Picos de Europa may be safely recommended as a rich and unworked field; and whenever virgin peaks of 8-9000 feet come to have an appreciable value in the climbing market, as I suppose some day they must, this district should not be overlooked by the enterprising speculator". Ormsby engaged one of the hunters who had accompanied Casiano to repeat the Llambrión ascent. This man lost the way among intricate ridges which "became shuffled with a multitude of other peaks". A burst of courage and confidence landed them on a summit that appears to have been the Te. Blanca (2617m.), but reference to a 1500 ft. cleft between them and the Llambrión suggests another view across the Jou de Trasllambrión which is seen at a greater distance from Pico Tesorero. Ormsby's account of the expedition was published in the Alpine Journal for 1872.

As late as 1891 the Comte de Saint-Saud failed to find the true top of the Llambrión. However, about the time of Ormsby's encounter with the labyrinth Spanish surveyors made the first ascent in 1870 of Pico Cortés, where a primary geodetic station was set up. A pillar raised on the Pico del Jierro in 1865 was abandoned in favour of the Cortés. This marked the

culmination of military surveying between 1861 and 1870 under the direction of Fernando Monet who had been primarily concerned with the periph-
eral zones. From this good vantage point in the eastern Andara massif
measurement and mapping work commenced over the region at large. Yet
progress was soon impeded by the crazy juxtaposition of ridges, for which
an accurate portrayal could only be charted by making observations from
within the terrain. Following publication in 1879 of a study for mineral
extraction in the Picos, the principal tracks for mules were constructed to
assist in mining operations.

There now came upon the scene a small group of French "pyreneists",
specialists dedicated to the study of the physical geography of the
Pyrenean range, and drawn to the Picos in the belief that the Cantabrian
cordillera was a simple extension of their investigations. Of course it
proved to be something quite different and was immensely more complicated.
After a few years they ceased to draw comparisons with and conclusions
from their Pyrenean experiences, and one of them devoted over 20 years
to unravelling the mysteries of this savage area. That he never completely
succeeded testifies to the magnitude of the task.

Aymar d'Arlot de Saint-Saud (1865-1936) commenced his systematic
study of the triple massif in 1890. A gentleman of means, he quickly
ingratiated himself with mining managers at Andara and so made his first
base there to explore the eastern massif; in this first year he scrambled to
the summits of several rocky towers, and along the main ridge to the Tabla
de Lechugales, apex of the group. In the central group immediately
opposite he also ascended the conspicuous Peña Vieja, at that time stead-
fastly argued by the miners to be the highest point in the Picos; it is now
the most frequently ascended peak and viewpoint in the entire region. In
1891 Saint-Saud was accompanied by Paul Labrouche; they missed the
Llambrión in poor visability but managed to get up the Tiro Llago by an
unorthodox route. Visiting the western massif for the first time they

25

searched for a means to cross from Te. Bermeja to the big Peña Santa and failed. Another attempt ended with an ascent of the lesser Peña Santa de Enol. The following year the same party imported a reputable Gavarnie guide and notched up several successes. The elusive Te. Cerredo, monarch of the region and spotted by Saint-Saud in 1890, was approached from Aliva in a vigorous enterprise lasting four days, over the Santa Ana and Arenizas Alta cols, and finally climbed on 30 July. Next day the Arenizas Baja col was crossed and the party stormed up the Llambrión after some dithering by the feeble local guides. Later in 1892 Labrouche with the guide F. Bernat-Sallés and a local man stole the coveted prize of the Peña Santa de Castilla. Picos Cortés and Pico de Santa Ana were among others attained in this season. Saint-Saud continued year after year in this manner. Everywhere he went he set up a small surveying station and worked with instruments for several hours. Most of his cartographic measurements were processed into mapping by Col. F. Prudent.

A visit by Albert Tissandier and two others in 1895 produced first recorded ascents of the imposing rock citadel called La Padiorna which overhangs Fuente Dé, and the Cornión Torre Blanca near the big Peña Santa.

Throughout this period excursions were begun, especially into the central massif, by southerly approaches - from Aliva, Fuente Dé-Liordes, and Valdeón. There is no written record of entry from the N or Cabrales side before the turn of the century - though shepherds and hunters must have been familiar with the ground for a long time. The Cares gorge was the chief deterrent; in those days the tiny dangerous track up it claimed the lives of natives every year. However the natural inlet to the central area is provided by the deep Bulnes valley, running due S and mounting directly to the base of the gigantic Naranjo in a daunting vertical interval of 1800m. At the end of the lower pastoral section is the quaint and remarkable hamlet of Bulnes (La Villa), built at two levels in the most amenable part of the valley. The trouble with route finding starts here and even today, with an improved path and waymarks, the best authorities on the region warn walkers and climbers alike against this approach. Between 1898 and 1908 a number of intrepid explorers struggled up the successive gorges of the Balcosin, Camburero and Jou Lluengo to the relatively spacious Vega de Urriello at the top; among them Pidal, Schulze, Fontan, Zabala, Victory, and an English woman, Constance Barnicott.

Almost as soon as the psychological barrier of the northern approach had been broken, Pedro Pidal, marqués de Villaviciosa de Asturias, and subsequently creator of the Covadonga-Corníon national park, put a plan to a particular Caín hunter who had the reputation of matching the agility of chamois on steep rock. Gregorio Pérez the hunter, nicknamed El Cainejo, had already reconnoitred the base of the Naranjo and advised his client that while the S wall was fairly short it looked steeper than the longer NE side where he proposed to make the attempt. To illustrate the fitness of this pair, the day before they bivouacked in the Camburero ravine they had climbed both Peña Santas in the western massif and reached their present site by descending across and climbing up the far side of the Cares gorge by the notoriously bad Trascamara-Collado de Cerredo trail, itself a rock climb and a miracle of route finding. For ordinary mortals such an expedition would amount to a three day trip, at least. Next day, 5 August, 1904, the NE face was tackled; it involved scaling walls and chimneys of grades IV+ and V- by today's reckoning, in a total height of 350m., and not surprisingly took them six hours. After an hour on the summit they party descended the same way, climbing down the very difficult pitches because abseiling and double rope down techniques were unknown in Spain; the primitive invention of the abseil was just being tried in the Alps. At once this tremendous feat becomes the outstanding event in Spanish mountaineering history; its boldness, the imagination and skill of its originators were not equalled for three decades. Indeed, the Naranjo was able to re-capture this preeminent position after the conquest of its magnificent W face in 1962, from which time it has been hailed as the Spanish Eiger.

Another "pyreneist" convert, L. Fontan de Négrin, translated the marquis' tale of the Naranjo conquest into French to introduce a wider audience. As if to endorse the calibre of this remarkable achievement, more or less the same route was repeated solo by the Munich climber and geologist Gustav Schulze on 1 October, 1906. Schulze was a fine technician, trained in the Northern Limestone ranges of Austria, and acquainted with roping down "dodges" and other experiments being carried out in this part of the Alps. But even he shrunk from the idea of reversing the NE face, and chose to come down the outer edge of the S face, mainly by primitive abseils. Already in 1906 the German had soloed the Peña Santa de Enol, the Tiro Tirso and Llambrión, and after his daring exploit on the Naranjo went on to the Cerredo and to make the first ascent of the Pico de los Cabrones. This last is possibly the most picturesque limestone mountain outside snowy regions anywhere in Europe and ranks among the first three or four most desirable peaks in the region; its normal route is grade III. But it was the Tiro Tirso that raised eyebrows, for Schulze went up the SE wall, grade III+/IV, and descended the easier W ridge - now the normal way. He seems to have been the Hermann Buhl of this era. This Munich climber returned in 1907 to ascend main summits in the Andara massif, and continued the following year to add new tops to his unique bag of summits.

The Naranjo was a springboard from which the Spaniards overtook foreigners in furthering exploration. This happened at much the same time as British dominance in the Alps began to wane. The story unfolds as a gradual awakening to the exceptional rock climbing possibilities in the Picos which were not fully realised until after World War Two. Among the names associated over a long period with this development are Alonso, Boada, Bustamante, Hernando, Landa, Lueje, Martinez, Odriozola, Régil, Rivas, Ubeda, Udaondo and many others.

After Ormsby's visit in 1870, the next British climbing party to appear on the scene is noted only in 1912 when D.W. Freshfield and W.P. Haskett-Smith made a short recce following a tour of the Pyrenees. W.R. Rickmers explored the Cantabrian chain in 1925 and remarked on the savage scenery and inaccessibility of the Picos, similarly W.T. Elmslie and two others in 1926, and the anglophile Paul Montadon in 1930. In the early thirties many British organised tourist parties visited Potes and the Aliva area and some of them must have ascended main summits nearby; the frequency of their names in hotel registers is commented upon by Elmslie when he made a second tour of the region. It was not until 1933 that a British party made any significant impact on the region. In that year A.W. Andrews arrived too early to be successful but G.F. Abercrombie and J.W. Cope followed two months later and managed to climb the Cerredo and Llambrión. Their failure to get up more than the first 60m. of the Naranjo on its NE side is vividly described in the Alpine Journal. Then nothing more is reported in English literature about the Picos until T.J. Fowle's party made the first British ascent of the Naranjo with Spanish companions in 1950.

A footnote and sign of the times can be appended. The 400m. W face direct of the Naranjo was climbed in 13 day-stages between late March and 16 May, 1974 by four Spaniards. The use of progressive seige tactics, a total of 220 pegs of which 90 were expansion bolts, and a liberal amount of fixed rope, led to widespread criticism outside Spain and a general feeling that this smooth monolithic face had been defiled. Recommendations about this face nowadays politely ignore the 1974 violation; ace climbers are directed to the original and meandering W face route of 1962 by E. Navarro and A. Rabada, which is held in high esteem and is considered in keeping with the tradition of Spanish mountaineering begun by Pidal and Pérez.

Two things have struck the author's Picos survey party teams most forcibly. The incredible amount of refuse and litter left lying about in the mountains and in the valley perimeters; and the large number of pegs to be found in all manner of rock climbs – although in 1980 there was evidence that a lot of these are being removed. Conservation and clean tactics as messages drummed across the European and American climbing scenes in the 1960s and 70s seem to have gone unheard in Spain. All this in an area which is still nearly as difficult of access as it was 50 years ago.

Naranjo de Bulnes from Camarmeña

Practical Considerations

ACCESS FROM BRITAIN

by Sea

Passenger and car ferry operates from Plymouth to Santander: Brittany
Ferries, Millbay Docks, Plymouth, Devon PL1 3EF. Tel:0752-21321.
The motor vessel Armorique carries 700 passengers and 170 cars, voyage
time 24 h. Departs Plymouth: Mondays 9.00am and Wednesdays 12.00 noon.
Returns from Santander: Tuesdays 11am and Thursdays 3.00pm. Times subject
to alteration. According to season, one way fares for passengers (with or
without cars) vary between £35-£40 for plain seating to £60-£80 for 2 berth
de luxe suite cabins; three intermediate stages of accommodation fares; all
meals extra. One way journey for average 1500cc family saloon car varies
from £50 in June to £95 in August, dropping to £50 again in September.
Reduction of 15% if vehicle is accompanied by three or more passengers.
Party group rates of 15% to 20% reduction on all prices, which are for 1980.

Passengers arriving in Santander and relying on public transport will find
rail and bus stations next to dock berth. As a rather tedious series of journeys is necessary by bus or train, or both, to reach Unquera, Panes and
Potes or Cangas de Onis, detailed inquiries should be made before leaving
home as to timetable and connections.

by Road

A wide choice of Channel crossings dictates the route followed across
France. Driving towards Biarritz the motorway system in France extends to
Poitiers. Bordeaux is avoidable by road systems on the E side. At Bayonne
Biarritz a motorway crosses the frontier near Hendaye to San Sebastián and
the A8 motorway (toll) continues to give a fast run to Bilbao. The complicated motorway ring round the S side of Bilbao presents no difficulty if signs
for Santander are followed. The motorway ends at Baracaldo, a densely
populated suburb with huge blast furnaces on the NW side of the sprawling
city. Here keep L and follow the tortuous painfully slow coastal corniche
road (N.634) with its continuous heavy traffic and caterpillar of lorries.
At the village of Solares keep L along the N.634 bis road (main road R for
Santander) to reach Vargas and Torrelavega, this last a fair-size town. The
latter section is quieter. After Torrelavega the main N.634 is taken to
Unquera; keep L along its bypass from which a not-too-distinct turning L is
made (by first moving R) to join the N.621 leading to Panes. In Panes
fork L to continue. This is the entry point from the E into the Picos de

Europa. For Cangas de Onis, in Panes turn sharp R where the L fork is for Potes. Allow 4 h. to drive from Bilbao to Panes.

An inland route between Bilbao and Panes/Potes or Riaño can be worked out from the map, through Valmaseda, Espinosa, Reinosa. This altogether more leisurely approach to the area takes 5-6 h. through countryside where mining, steel works and petro-chemical plants are absent.

Visitors coming from the S, e.g. Madrid, should avoid the badly congested N.630 between León and Oviedo. After Zamora or Valladolid take the N.601 towards León and leave it to follow the N.621 to Cistierna and Riaño. A tunnelled motorway is scheduled to be constructed along the bad section referred to. Indeed the N coast road beyond Bilbao is due to have a motorway built and an outline of its route appears on the current Firestone road map.

frontier at Hendaye (Behobie)		0 km.
Bilbao	116	116
Solares	90	206
Vargas	22	228
Torrelavega	10	238
Unquera	52	290
Panes	11	301

by Air

Iberia Airways and British Airways run daily flights from London Heathrow to Bilbao (Sondica). Flying time, $1\frac{1}{2}$ h. Tourist economy fare valid 7-30 days in 1980 = £140 return in summer season (cut price tickets from £90). Flights are often delayed by a persistent fog/smog over the Bilbao industrial area. The airport (Sondica) is situated about 8 km. N of city. Frequent buses, or taxi, to city centre and bus/railway terminals. In view of the commercial traffic along the Bilbao-Santander road (see above), the rail journey is preferable to the "express" bus service. After Santander, see comments at end of section for travelling by sea to Santander, above. Note: Iberia is scheduled to remove itself to London Gatwick, and the Sondica airport is scheduled for removal to Vitoria, some 65 km. S of Bilbao, though connected by a motorway for most of this distance. When this change takes place approaches to the Picos will alter radically.

Fly/Drive

For a party of three or four this is the most economical and convenient way to visit the Picos de Europa. Iberia and British Airways operate the European fly/drive scheme to Bilbao. The cost varies according to month and number travelling in a party, but is confined to 2, 3 or 4 persons per car. Four categories of car are available, rising in price according to size/class of vehicle. A typical example for 1980: 3 persons taking a Category 2 car

(Fiat 127 or Ford Fiesta) for 2 weeks in September = £170 per person incl-
usive of air travel by scheduled flights, car hire and insurance; free mileage.
Cars are collected at airport reception and returned there on departure.
Petrol tanks are full on taking delivery and this is paid for in cash at Bilbao
reception. Petrol (gasolina) remaining in tank after returning car is calcul-
ated and refunded in cash. An international driving licence is advisable
for Spain though not strictly mandatory. A British full licence is required.
Two persons may be nominated for driving. All documentation is completed
and payment made at the British end. A handout town plan available at
Bilbao reception for leaving the airport and finding the way into and out of
the city is quite inadequate. The following directions may assist car drivers.

The Sondica airport access road is only 200m. long. At the bottom turn
sharp R into a main road and follow this W to an island junction at a bend.
Turn L and follow a dual carriageway corniche road which eventually
descends to filter with traffic lights into a broad three-lane carriageway
leading to the city. Continue on this for a short way and bear R with the
traffic mainstream across a wide bridge over the river. About 300m. further
a traffic island/roundabout system appears. Before this turn sharp R after
the bridge down a short road/ramp which filters into another road coming
from the R alongside the river. Drive to the next roundabout (Sagrado
Corazón) and go straight across. Continue for 100m. to the first turning R
(Santander sign). Follow a zigzag course through broad backstreets with
Santander signs to a T junction. Turn R into a main road which is the N.634
and follow this without possible error past the Baracaldo junction at end of
motorway, to continue in the Santander direction. Crowded, busy road.
See section above for additional comments.

In the reverse direction, on reaching the outskirts at Baracaldo fork R on
to motorway and follow this to the first turn off possible, marked Bilbao
West (you move off R and overpass to bear L). This leads without deviation
to the large Sagrado Corazón roundabout. Go along the road ahead,
passing the one-way ramp from the bridge, and take the next turning R to
make a simple circling movement R to join the bridge road at a higher
level where the outward route is joined.

CURRENCY, REGULATIONS AND HUTS

The unit of currency in Spain is the Peseta. The Sterling rate of exchange
in 1980 averaged Pesetas 173 = £1.00 Passports are required for entering
the country but no certificates of vaccination are needed.

Club Huts

The few FEM huts, and others, in the Picos mountain region that may have
wardens will give visitors a discount on production of a current members'

card issued by an international mountaineering body affiliated to the reciprocal rights scheme for the Alps and elsewhere. It is not generally understood that this scheme extends well beyond the Alps and is valid for instance in Eastern Europe, Spain, Greece and several parts of the African continent. Most important of all a card obtains a substantial discount on the Fuente Dé cablecar.

Hut charges are very modest, less than half those imposed in the Alps. At all huts without a warden no charge is payable, assuming the door is unlocked. If it is ascertained in the valley that a door may be locked, the keyholder will normally ask for a refundable deposit, or in the case of a part time wardened hut a fee as well, possibly payable after returning the key. In August and September huts without wardens are normally open and keys need not be sought. Sometimes a fee payable will be displayed as a notice in the hut, together with an address where the fee should be sent. Visitors are asked to respect these instructions. If in any doubt about the hut situation, in Potes contact the photographic shop Bustamante.

GRADING OF ROUTES AND CLIMBS

These are based on the international summer system for rock climbing, roman numerals I to VI, and qualified for more accuracy by minus (-) and (+) signs; thus II-, II, II+ is the rising order through grade II. At the bottom of the scale absolutely safe paths for walking without particular steepness but possibly quite loose underfoot come into the lowest category, I-. Level grade I involves terrain often without paths and steep loose sections mixed with scrambling. In I+ there will be short moderately difficult stretches on rock where experienced mountain walkers/scramblers should not need a rope. A rope may be needed at the level of II-, especially if steep frozen snow is encountered, while at level grade II technical climbing in the proper sense begins. Grade III equates to "Just Very Difficult" in British rock climbing parlance; grade IV to "Just Severe", grade V to "Just Very Severe", grade VI to "Hard Very Severe", all free climbing standards without resort to pegs for aid while pegs may be needed for belaying, etc.

ACCESS VALLEYS

Starting on N side of the region and working clockwise round it, valleys and entry points into various parts of the massif are given parish district names as follows.

Cabrales (= ewe's milk cheese): Arenas de Cabrales (145m.) – Puente Poncebos (new inn, 225m.). Metalled road except for last 300m. after bridge on L going up to Sotres. New inn is at precise entrance to the Garganta del Cares.

Roman bridge at Cangas de Onis. Drawing by Fonrémis from a photo by Saint-Saud

<u>Aliva</u>: (1) S approach. From Espinama (877m. in Liébana district) – Duje/ Nevandi saddle (1472m.) – Aliva hut/hotel (1667m.). Jeep road with 1 in 4 gradients.

(2) N approach. As for Cabrales to Puente Poncebos, then cross bridge L to pass below Tielve hamlet (691m.) and reach roadhead by steep zigzags to Sotres hamlet (1060m.). Metalled road, parts in need of repair in 1980. At foot of last zigzags a rough jeep road fork R up main valley to join (1) at saddle below hut/hotel. Land Rover services at Espinama and Sotres for both approaches.

<u>Liébana</u>: Panes (40m.) – La Hermida (98m.) – Potes (291m.) – Espinama (877m.) – Fuente Dé (1090m., cableway and roadhead with large carpark). Metalled road. Fuente Dé – Balcón del Cable (1843/1855m.), public cablecar service, cheap by Alpine standards and with good reduction for visitors with current alpine club cards. 10am–8pm in summer.

<u>Valdeón</u>: (1) S approach. Portilla de la Reina (1231m.) – Puerto de Pande-trave (1562m.)– Santa Marina de Valdeón (1158m.), good metalled road. From here a single track metalled farm road descends to the main centre of Posada de Valdeón (940m.). This road continues metalled but narrow down to the Mirador del Tombo (866m.) just passed Cordiñanes, a monument to first president of the FEM, the architect J.D. Ubeda, creator of mountain huts in the Picos and in the rest of Spain; a little lower you pass a wolf trap which has been in use for over 300 years. Beyond the Mirador a new tarmac surface allows private cars to continue through the upper Cares gorge, very narrow single track with some risk from stonefall/accident, to Caín (513m.). Not recommended to nervous drivers, short sections of 1 in 5. Land Rover service from Posada de Valdeón.

(2) SW approach. Cangas de Onis (87m.) or Riaño (1048m.) to El Pontón col (1298m.) – Puerto de Panderruedas/Mirador de Santa Maria del Villar (1450m.) – Posada de Valdeón. Good asphalt road all the way, then as for (1) down to Caín.

<u>Dobra</u>: Cangas de Onis (87m.) – Sella gorge road turn off at Oseja de Sajambre (760m.) – Soto de Sajambre (950m.), asphalt road. Continuation by jeep road feasible for cars to the Vegabaño hut/restaurant (1340m.).

<u>Onis</u>: Cangas de Onis (87m.) – Covadonga (257m.) – Lago Enol/Ercina (1108m.). Metalled road to large carpark area below motel. Before this pt. and just before reaching the first (Enol) lake, unmarked jeep road turning on R can be followed by cars for 3 km. towards the Vega Redonda hut. Carpark on R after saddle 1086m. Near latter pt. ignore a road R.

<u>Liébana – Valdeón direct connection</u>. Between Fuente Dé (metalled road head) and the Puerto de Pandetrave a big track suitable for jeeps only now crosses the Valcavao col (1782m.). Land Rover hire at Espinama. The latter col, not named on any map at present, is found 700m. W of the

grassy summit called Alto de la Triguera (1914m.) and immediately below
a knoll of 1814m. which divides our col from another of 1783m. This connection is scheduled to be upgraded to a metalled road. When the work is
complete it will have a profound and inevitably detrimental effect on the
unique Valdeón. The social and commercial importance of this link has
unqualified support in the area.

TOWNS, VILLAGES AND BASE CENTRES

Arenas de Cabrales   145m.

Pleasant village resort, main services, several hotels/pensions, bank.
Bus to: Panes, 23 km. Cangas de Onis, 28 km. Puente Poncebos, 7 km.
Taxi hire for Sotres.

Puente Poncebos   225m.

No services. Hotel beside generating station on R with small shop. New
inn with restaurant 600m. further on unmade road at entrance to Cares
gorge. Limited bus service from Arenas (above).

Sotres   1060m.

Hamlet above Duje valley, 18 km. from Arenas de Cabrales; taxi hire
from latter via Poncebos. Small inns with restaurant service, Land Rover
hire, no other services. Very rural and quaint.

Panes   40m.

Rather drab large village, main services, small hotels. Bus to: Arenas de
Cabrales, 23 km. Unquera, 11 km. (Santander, 79 km.). Potes, 27 km.

Potes   291m.

Large village resort, perhaps the best in the region, convivial atmosphere,
all main services, 7 hotels, several pensions, apartments to rent. Main
public campsite with good facilities situated 3 km. outside on road to
Espinama. Potes lies on the edge of the rain shadow and misses most of the
inclement weather rolling in from the NW over the Picos region. Bus to
Panes, 27 km. Espinama, 20 km. and Fuente Dé, 24 km. To Puerto de
San Glorio, 27 km., Portilla de la Reina, 37 km., Riaño, 56 km.

Espinama   877m.

Small hamlet 20 km. from Potes, two pensions, small shop, café/bars.
Land Rover hire centre.

Fuente Dé   1090m.

Roadhead from Potes, 24 km. Bus service. Huge carpark with water fountain ("God's Fountain") and bar/restaurant at cableway station. Just below
cableway on same side of road, modest inn and restaurant. On opposite
side of road, huge state owned hotel (parador) with dormitory accommodation. Camping on grassland adjoining, officially near the parador using
their toilet/washing facilities, or further away under copses with no
facilities. The entire camping area, which is large, was in a filthy condition in 1980. Ample water from cableway carpark. No other services.
Cableway operates every 10 min. between 10am and 8pm until end Sept.
Top station at 1843m., the most popular entry into the Picos.

Portilla de la Reina   1231m.

Hamlet with one pension and small foodshop. Infrequent bus to: Santa
Marina de Valdeón, 15 km. Riaño, 19 km. Potes, 37 km.

Santa Marina de Valdeón   1158m.

Hamlet with one pension. Infrequent bus from Portilla de la Reina, 15 km.
Narrow metalled road (taxi) to Posada de Valdeón, 4 km.

Posada de Valdeón   940m.

Charming, picturesque village base, the most unspoiled to date in the
Picos. One hotel, three inn/pensions, two small shops. Approached
from Santa Marina (above), or more usually from the Puerto del Pontón,
14 km. along new metalled road over the Panderruedas col (no bus service).

Caín   513m.

For access, see Valdeón Access Valleys above. Primitive hamlet with
lodging house (Casa de Matilde) in unique setting, simple meals possible.

Riaño   1048m.

Village with 4 small hotels and limited services/shopping. Ski centre
development underway. 2 km. outside, a state owned parador (hotel) was
closed in 1979. Bus to: Potes, 56 km. Cangas de Onis, 68 km.

Soto de Sajambre   950m.

Agreeable hamlet, one hotel, two pensions, limited services. Two hotels
below at Oseja. Infrequent bus from Cangas de Onis, 50 km. Riano, 27 km.

Cangas de Onis   87m.

City of Onis, formerly capital of the Asturian kings. Interesting historical town, all main services, numerous hotels and pensions. Bus to: Covadonga, 10 km. Santander, 133 km. Oviedo, 73 km.

Covadonga   257m.

Long Cave. Village and shrine dominated by its monumental red basilica standing on a promontory and commemorating the battle for Christianity against the Moors in 722, visited by many pilgrims, jammed full of people in the peak month of September. Limited services, two modest and one grand hotel. Frequent bus from Cangas de Onis, 10 km.

Lago Enol/Ercina   1108m.

Enol = lake without issue. Roadhead about 12 km. from Covadonga, bus service. One motel (1120m.) with good restaurant, another separate café off road between the two lakes.

Note: Experience with restaurants shows that while most of these are part of hotels (Cangas de Onis excepted), it is rarely possible to eat outside of fairly rigid meal times. Breakfast can seldom be had before 9am, lunch before one pm, dinner before 9pm. Between times meals are not served. Snacks might be obtained in more numerous café/bars.

A cheap local dish and restaurant meal is fabada which might contain variable ingredients from day to day, but always including beans; it is filling but not very appetising. Vegetables are a luxury but green salad can be eaten at most meals. Fish soup is a speciality of the region and can be recommended. Fish dishes are cheaper than most. Local cheeses are rather dry and crumbly but acceptable enough.

HUTS AT BASE CENTRES OR APPROACHABLE BY JEEP ROADS

Aliva   1667m.

Owned by the State Tourist Board and managed like a hotel with a good restaurant service; 46 places in single and double rooms, h & c water, baths, etc., open June–end September. No reduced rates for club card holders.

Below Sotres, rough jeep road commences at foot of final tarmac zigzags to hamlet, and is followed up the Duje valley. Only suitable for small cars with high ground clearance. On foot, $2\frac{1}{2}$ h. From Espinama, as for Sotres; road on this side very steep and rough in places, not generally possible for cars. On foot, $2\frac{1}{2}$–3 h. From Fuente Dé cableway top station, jeep road over the Covarrobres col (1930m.), 45 min. on foot. Land Rover service on all three routes.

Cableway Hut   1843m.

At top of Fuente Dé cableway, part of restaurant facility, privately owned, simple meals in daytime only, 18 sleeping places.

Fuente Dé Hut   1050m.

On W side of Parador near cableway station. Privately owned, 9 places with kitchen, door locked, key at Junta Vecinal in Espinama.

Albergue de Vegabaño   1340m.

Owned by the León local authority, all mod. cons., inside running water, places for 25, simple restaurant service when warden in residence. Otherwise door locked and keys at main inn in Soto de Sajambre. Reached from latter hamlet by jeep road passable for cars, or 1 h. on foot. Taxi hire.

Casa Municipal de Pastores   1080m.

Situated 800m. along the jeep road branching S from the Covadonga-Enol metalled road just before reaching the Enol lake (conspicuous unmarked turn-off). Owned by the Oviedo local authority, from whom a pass-ticket is needed to stay at hut. Otherwise the warden will permit one night stop-overs for internationally federated club card holders, vacancies permitting. Simple restaurant service or self cooking, places for 30.

LAND ROVER HIRE FOR JEEP ROADS

Land Rover taxi/hire services are operated by local mining companies and some innkeepers. Most of the vehicles are relatively new and of the long wheelbase kind, capable of carrying 9 passengers and luggage. Unless a party exceeds six in number to share the charge, or a smaller party can combine with another to make up numbers, all Land Rover trips are very expensive. With a full load the shared cost is quite reasonable. The services most useful for mountain parties are as follows:

Sotres to Aliva hut.
Sotres to Andara mines.
La Hermida to Andara mines.
Espinama to Aliva hut, continuation possible over Covarrobres col to top of Fuente Dé cableway, or to La Vueltona.
Fuente Dé cableway top station to Aliva hut, or to La Vueltona.
Espinama to Pandetrave road pass over the Valcavao grassland col.
Other possible routes are noted in previous descriptions in this section of the guide.

PRACTICAL CAMPSITES AT BASE CENTRES

Camping at the undermentioned places which all have good sites for tents can be undertaken with discretion. If in doubt about where to pitch a tent, inquire at the nearest habitation. All have fountains or stream water nearby unless otherwise stated. Use water from springs/fountains and not streams whenever possible. Facilities such as toilets and wash-ups for campers are indicated at sites marked with an asterisk.

Puente Poncebos (beyond new inn, beside Cares river); Sotres (beside Duje river below hamlet); Andara mines (anywhere in cwm with spring); Potes* (official campsite with services 3 km. along road towards Fuente Dé); Aliva (excellent sites on grass above and below hut/hotel, popular); Fuente Dé* (W of cableway carpark and beside copse); Hoyo de Lloroza (behind top station of Fuente Dé cableway, water probable in last but one hollow to N, 20 min.); Posada de Valdeón (seek local advice); Puerto de Panderruedas (anywhere); Vegabaño hut* (anywhere); Enol/Ercina lakes (numerous spacious sites; fountains; in the Redonda hut direction note that the Redemuña stream at end of jeep road, bridge (Pozo del Alemán) is normally dry or dirty in summer).

MOUNTAIN CAMPING AND BIVOUACS

Lightweight camping is possible anywhere above base camp areas without restriction. However there are few places above 1800m. where tents can be pitched satisfactorily because of the rocky nature of the terrain. A more realistic proposition is a bivouac under a large jutting block or in a cave. A number of these with shelter walls and clean floors can be found throughout the region and some are noted in later descriptions.

TOURIST DEVELOPMENTS

An ambitious plan exists to "open up" the Murallón de Amusa - the S wall of the Cares gorge. The road at Puente Poncebos would be extended up the N side of the gorge along terraces followed by the main path and the higher Canal de la Electra del Viesgo, probably as far as the Caseta del Sayo huts. Cableways at two points would then be hung across the gorge to reach the top of the wall, some 1200m. high. The shelving plateau atop the wall might give limited opportunities for winter skiing but the project seems to rest on the value as a summer tourist attraction and viewpoint. Mechanical assistance as such would reduce the ascent of the Cerredo to a rather long one day trip. Mountain walkers would benefit with a starting point at 1450m. while rock climbers could tackle several groups of towers rarely visited at present. It would also offer a shorter route to the Ubeda hut by utilising one of the passes over the Pardida-Albo ridge. The economics of this scheme seem to indicate that many years will elapse before it comes to fruition. See also notes on the Cabrones hut in next section of the guide.

Associated with this project is a small road to be made all the way up the Cares gorge between Poncebos and Caín. The technical difficulties are considerable, and while the vertical interval over the 12 km. distance of this famous garganta is only 300m., many ups and downs will have to be negotiated in the cliffs. The water conduit following the L bank of the gorge already passes through 100 tunnels. This project on completion is presumably one for Land Rover type vehicles only.

Finally, a scheme exists for extending the Fuente Dé cableway. From the present top station another section would stretch to the Colladina de las Nieves and/or Pico de la Padiorna. This would greatly reduce the hard walk from Fuente Dé to the Jermoso hut and enable a scenic circuit to be made on foot in a day from Fuente Dé.

BIBLIOGRAPHY AND MAPS

In modern times no books have been published in English which describe the Picos de Europa in detail; none in French, Italian or German, except for the latter a chapter of 20 pages in Bergwelt Spaniens, A. Jolis (J.Fink Verlag, Stuttgart, 1973). All current literature is in Spanish and most of this is in booklets giving a picture summary of the region.

A new climbing guide (the latest in a long line) was published in Spanish in 1980. Los Picos de Europa, M.A. Adrados, J. López (privately, in Oviedo). Notwithstanding its 400 pages and separate map pocket, it is a selection of about one quarter of recorded routes (this about 1/10th of all routes to date), and many descriptions are severely abbreviated. Moreover there are no approach descriptions, leaving the user to find his own way from hut, etc. to foot of route. The guide is otherwise excellent for the rock technician but it assumes that he already has a considerable knowledge of the region.

A well produced and attractive picture guide is Los Picos de Europa, J.R. Lueje (Editorial Everest, León, 5th ed. 1980). It has brief textual descriptions and no technical information on rock climbing (but a lot of suggestive hints).

Spanish mountaineering club publications going back nearly 80 years contain the progressive history of exploration and development. More substantial publications date from the late 19th century. Among the latter are two classic works of interest to mountain walkers and climbers; <u>Picos de Europa</u>, P.Pidal, J.F. Zabala, Madrid, 1918; <u>Monographie des Picos de Europa</u>, Comte de Saint-Saud, Paris, 1922 (in French, reprinted 1937). Both are very hard to come by; only half a dozen copies of the latter are known to exist in Britain.

For the present work about 30 articles in British, French and German mountain journals have been traced. The earliest description in English about the real nature of the massif appears in the Alpine Journal, Vol.6, 1872, an article on the mountains of Spain by John Ormsby.

The current mountain journal containing most information on new developments is Pyrenaica, a quarterly published by the Federación Vasca de Montaña (Basque mountain federation) in Bilbao; its English correspondent is Txomin Uriarte. He recently described the problem of producing a definitive up to date guide for the region, which would entail issuing several large volumes, as "very difficult if not impossible".

Maps

The official survey in Spain (IGC) has not produced new large scale mapping of the area for many years. All available maps are private association or commercial productions based on original IGC work and updated according to the ability of editors and designer/artists. In consequence none of the mapping is of a high standard, as exampled by that now obtainable for British mountain areas and the Alps. The best are those produced by the Federación Española de Montañismo (FEM), Madrid. In their 25m. series only one sheet is in print at present, but the others should become available again soon. This and other maps are as follows.

1/25,000 Picos de Europa. FEM.
1. Macizo Oriental, 1978, panoramas on reverse side. Also sold with a large booklet.
2. Macizo Central, 1968, out of print, under revision.
3. Macizo Occidental, to be published.

1/25,000 Picos de Europa. EA, Granollers.
1. Macizo Occidental, includes a 28 page booklet guide.
2. Macizos Central y Oriental, includes a 28 page booklet guide.

1/30,000 Picos de Europa. Javier Malo, Baracaldo.
Sh. A-32. Macizos Central y Oriental, 1974. Kammkarte with panoramas, technical data and route gradings on reverse side.

1/50,000 National grid sheets (old series) IGC.
Sh. 55,56,80,81.
1/50,000 Picos de Europa. Mapa de los tres macizos. FEM. 7th.ed. 1978. Panorama and descriptions on reverse side.

1/50,000 Mapa de los tres macizos de Picos de Europa.
Multicolour kammkarte, the most easily read of all maps. FAM, Oviedo.
2nd.ed. 1980. Available separately and sold as part of the new 1980
climbing guide noted on previous page.

1/200,000 Costa Verde-Picos de Europa. Sh. T-21. Cornisa Cantábrica.
Sh. T-22. Firestone tourist and road maps.

Maps from IGC of 1/200,000 are also available, and while contoured are
considered much less useful than the Firestone ones. Road maps of scale
1/500,000 are numerous.

Maps listed above are generally available from West Col Productions.

Altitudes and Cartographic Standards

In the opinion of the writer, and others, many heights accepted for a long
time in the Picos are suspect. More than that, they must be wrong. Errors
amounting to as much as 100m. have been noted by the author's parties.
In 1980 the author met a surveying team bound for the Llambrión and
Cerredo with the purpose of re-measuring both summits; it is now thought
that the difference in height between the two peaks is 25m. and not the
long established 6m. More positive indication of altitude errors are too
numerous to mention, but those which may seriously affect the outcome of
a route are cited in the guide.

Even more serious are cartographic errors (one map is copied from another
and thus mistakes are perpetuated), especially in the position of cols and
secondary ridges extending from main ones. Some ridges go in the wrong
direction. Dotted "path" lines, though often with no path on the ground,
indicate ridge crossings at the wrong point, and so on. These also are too
numerous to list but most of those known to the author's parties are correct-
ed in descriptions which follow.

Picos de Europa from Mirador de Llesba

MOUNTAIN HUTS

EASTERN (ANDARA) MASSIF

There are no huts in this area. Good campsites near the jeep road crossing the Andara mines area at 1900m. between Sotres and La Hermida offer excellent base for excursions. Good biv. cave at foot of Pico del Castillo del Grajal (2052m.), on its N side near jeep road at head of Canal de las Vacas, and opposite site of old Mazarrasa mines. This is slightly above the Pozo de Andara (dry tarn) and close to a spring. Note: Pico Cortés is more conveniently approached from the Aliva (W) side.

CENTRAL (URRIELES) MASSIF

Verónica Bivouac Hut   2325m.

FEM. Hut shell is a dismantled radar turret from an aircraft carrier, originally taken to site as a joke by local climbers. Small aluminium shelter for 4, table and stools, no other equipment. Water from snowmelt 80m. to rear. Situated on a rib at SE foot of P. Tesorero and about 400m. distance SW of the sheer wall below the Te. de Horcados Rojos. Door normally open late summer, otherwise keys at Potes chemist shop. Overflow biv. sites to rear and below, uncomfortable.

1.   From Aliva hut (1667m.) by jeep road to Horcadina de Covarrobres (1930m.) and by same road NW to sharp Vueltona bend (1920m.) (1 h.). Jeep hire possible to this pt. Good biv. boulder cave 20m. below bend; fountain/snow patch 80m. up L side of boulder bed above. To this pt. by connecting jeep road from Fuente Dé cableway (1843m.), 35 min. From bend continue up stony trail (Sendero Bustamante) NW to obvious Canalona junction on R (2275m.), 45 min. Keep to main trail now in horizontal sections working W to pass below fine cliffs (small spring near cave above) and by a short ascent reach a small saddle still some distance from the Rojos col (30 min.).

Leave trail and ascend a small track L (SW) up grassy rocks;
open bivs. and small campsites; by keeping slightly R a rocky
track goes up a gutter to skyline dry stonewall at top. Here
turn L and descend L side of rib crest to hut (15 min., $2\frac{1}{2}$ h.
from Aliva hut, 2 h. from cableway).

2. <u>Canal de la Jenduda</u> = great crack/slit. Examined from
Fuente Dé, the first and most obvious gully high up in the
continuous upper rock wall seen L of the cableway. It gives
access to the plateau above in the Hoyo de Lloroza where R. 1
is joined. Originally the only practical direct way for pedes-
trians from Fuente Dé into the central massif. The cableway
supersedes it; when the latter breaks down (not infrequent in
recent years) it still receives numerous ascents. Or the
impecunious, wishing to avoid the alternative Espinama-Aliva
Landrover service, will adopt it.

The gully, narrow all the way with an average angle of 37°,
is enclosed by impressive walls. Where the terrain permits
there is a tight zigzag track in the bed. Boulder pitch at mid-
height turned by an 8m. staircase on R side; 2 or 3 other gravel
covered slab pitches. Grade I. Very hard work with a sack.
Interesting and worthwhile in descent. Access to gully entrance
is from contractor's cableway path seen slanting generally R
below the upper precipices. Leave this at an almost horizontal
zag L, which is taken away from the cableway path; it soon
rises trending L by a poor track overgrown with grass which
is followed steeply L to foot of gully. Fuente Dé to plateau,
$2\frac{1}{2}$-$3\frac{1}{2}$ h. In descent, $1\frac{1}{2}$ h. Vertical interval 800m., gully
proper, 275m.

<u>Julian Delgado Ubeda Hut</u>   2050m.

FEM. Ubeda was first president of FEM and the initiator of
mtn. huts in Spain. Fine stone built hut, part time warden, 40
places with recent extension, cooking utensils, butane stove,
but take your own. Water fountain 70m. to rear with piped

extension to hut. Door normally open late summer. Keys at
Potes (chemist), Poncebos (inn), Posada de Valdeón (police).
Situated at edge of the Vega de Urriello, below W face of the
Naranjo de Bulnes. Not an easy hut to reach from any direction.
Good campsites closeby.

From S:

3.   Across <u>Horcados Rojos</u> (2330, 2345m.), L. As for R. 1 to
small saddle in main trail. Continue into last hollow (snow)
below Rojos col. Ascend to within 200m. distance of lowest pt.
of col, on L. Leave main trail and go up a rocky track half L
towards ridge coming down from Los Urrielles (2501m.), a
craggy shoulder in front of P. Tesorero. Ascend steeply to a
ridge gap behind shoulder/step above col (30 min.). On the
other side descend a steep narrow gully to scree and cross L to
a wall. Continue below this and zigzag down loose ground to
cross horizontally into a narrow rock gully. Descend this to
more loose zags, bearing R (facing out) to drop over slabby bands
into a short gully/ramp leading to a better track running horiz-
onally under N wall of the Rojos col to join the direct way.
Steep snow patches to end July. (30 min.).

Alternatively, more delicate, shorter and direct. Continue
to the Rojos col; keep to a track bearing R and reach a grassy
shoulder up to R (2345m.). Here the track bears R up broad
ridge slope towards the Torre. Ignore an initial horizontal
track L (desperate false trail). Take a second one L about 25m.
higher; this rises slightly under broken cliffs supporting the
ridge. It soon descends gradually over bad ground, old paint
marks, where track is difficult to follow and where there are
no projections for security over a distance of 200m.; gravel on
earth and slabs at 35°; ice axe useful. Continue this delicate
descending traverse which returns L down steep broken ribs
and gullies, soon going straight down with much loose rock to
scree and grass at the bottom and junction with other route over
col (45 min.).

A level path now runs N, adjoining the Boches hoyo, to top of a step above the Sin Tierra hoyo. A steep descent and a descending traverse along a good path leads to N end of latter hoyo. Cross a grassy shoulder, up and down, with a final short ascent to hut (45 min.; from Verónica hut, $1\frac{3}{4}$-2 h. From cableway, $3\frac{1}{2}$-4 h. From Aliva hut, 4-$4\frac{1}{2}$ h. In reverse direction, hut to Rojos col, $2\frac{1}{4}$ h.).

4.   Across the Co. Santa Ana (2488m.). Considered by some as an alternative for avoiding the unpleasant N side of the Rojos col, but not worth the effort. Can be done from the Aliva hut, up the Vidrio gully to the Canalona col, then by a traverse under the Santa Ana peak. Or from the cableway top station/Verónica biv. hut via good track to the Canalona col; all described elsewhere. The descent of W side of the Santa Ana col to path beside the Boches hoyo (R. 3) is steep, stony, tedious and mostly trackless. At least $1\frac{1}{2}$ h. longer than regular ways over the Rojos col.

From N:

5.   Puente Poncebos inn, Jaya bridge, Bulnes (La Villa, 695m., $1\frac{1}{4}$ h., small inn with 20 dormitory places), Balcosin ravine, Camburero ravine, Jou Lluengo to broad entrance under Celada ravine. Continue keeping R below this up to hut. Path has been much improved but needs care to follow correctly in several places. A long hard ascent of 1800m., only for parties in good training ($5\frac{1}{2}$-7 h.). Better for descent ($3\frac{1}{2}$ h.).

6.   A longer alternative at an easier angle, though marred by a poor track and route finding problems. Take L branch of the river fork below Balcosin ravine and go up pleasantly E to the Co. de Pandébano (1224m.). Now ascend S with a good trail to the Terenosa huts (1330m., 3 h., FAM hut here with 30 places, keys at Puente Poncebos new inn). From here a vague high level track contours to the Co. Vallejo (1650m.), a shoulder in a broad ridge. On the other side descend a steep rough gully, delicate, into a ravine and continue round spurs and across

trackless ravines to round a final spur where a descent leads
to foot of Celada ravine near hut (4¼ h. from Terenosa).

From E:

7.   Sotres to Co. de Pandébano by a mule trail; it branches
W from the Aliva jeep road below Sotres to cross Duje river.
Then to the Terenosa hut (1¾ h.) where R. 6 is joined.

Cabrones Hut   2080m.
FEM. New in 1979, replaces former J.R. Lueje biv. hut
destroyed by a blizzard in 1970. Location wrongly marked on
most maps. Places for 24, table, benches, summary cooking
utensils. Keys kept in summer by head shepherd at the Majada
Amuesa huts above Bulnes, also at Poncebos inn. Situated
100m. from fountain in the Jou de los Cabrones, below N side
of peak of same name. A long, hard walk.

8.   Puente Poncebos inn, Jaya bridge, Bulnes (see R. 5); before
latter village cross the Colines bridge R and climb zigzag trail
to the upper Bulnes hamlet (Ariba, 700m.). Continue by same
trail W up a deep side valley, a ravine at the top, to the Amuesa
huts further N (1418m., 3¼ h., FAM dormitory with 20 places,
keys with head shepherd at nearby huts and at Puente Poncebos
new inn. Water at top of Amuesa ravine). Above these pastures
a broad grassy spur becoming rocky higher up rises due S.
Follow a track with cairns up this to 1950m., large marker rock
and waymarks, where it bears L to cross rough hollows and
gullies of scree and blocks, and goes up a ridge below the pinnacled Trave chain on R. It later crosses a saddle and descends
into the Jou de los Coches. Follow bed of valley system S into
next hoyo, the Jou de los Cabrones, where hut is found against
the rear side. Intermittent paint flashes all the way (6½ h. from
Poncebos inn).

Collado Jermosa Hut   2064m.
FEM. Fine little hut constructed on saddle of same name at a
veritable deadend below W face of the Llambrión group. 12

places, kitchen, etc., part time warden, door normally open late summer, or keys at Potes (chemist) and S. Marina de Valdeón. Water 100m. distance.

9.   From head of Fuente Dé cableway (1843m.), go along jeep road for 7 min., then move L (W) down grassy rib alongside the Lloroza hoyo. After a few min. a good track is picked up to enter the valley rising W as the Canal de San Luis. Reach a fork and keep L. The track works back R to the entrance of a ravine. Climb a spur up to L (cairns) and continue to a grassy depression then the Ca. de las Nieves (2226m.). On the other side descend scree and grass to track coming from the Ca. de la Padiorna (1930m.). This track rises along the R (E) side of a long trench called the Sedo de la Padiorna then contours round a cwm (Llago Cimero) to ascend steeply L followed by a traverse horizontally under the Llambrión group. Cross a series of ribs, Las Colladinas, and continue horizontally, passing above the fountain, to hut ($4\frac{1}{2}$ h. from cableway, $5\frac{1}{4}$ h. from Aliva hut). Much the best way on this side.

10.   From Fuente Dé the above approach can be joined at the Padiorna saddle by following a big mule trail up the Tornos de Liordes ravine to the Co. de Liordes (1958m.), then taking the highest track on R (N) side round the Vega de Liordes to saddle at W end of this large pasture and former mining area. In centre, ruined workings and fountain; forestry hut in SW corner ($3\frac{1}{2}$ h. to saddle, 6 h. to hut).

11.   From Cordiñanes hamlet (880m.) below Posada de Valdeón, by the Rienda path into Asotin gorge, and by L (N) exit up the very steep and partly trackless Argallo Cangosto ravine to join the previous trails just beyond Las Colladinas ($3-3\frac{1}{2}$ h.). Hard work with a sack.

12.   From S. Marina de Valdeón, the most comfortable route for those with a car. On main road above hamlet park in small

space at 1400m. on S side of stream bed coming down from the
Co. de Valdeón, where path crosses road. Ascend path working
further away and S of bed, steep for 300m., to join a traverse
path coming from the Pandetrave col, which mounts gradually
L to the Valdeón col (1775m.). Cross this E and traverse by a
good path past a fountain to zigzags in the Canal de Pedavejo,
rising plainly to the Co. de Remoña (2030m.). Descend the N
side in more zigzags for 100m., passing forestry hut, to reach
the Vega de Liordes and Padiora saddle where R. 9, 10 are
joined (4 h. from road parking to hut).

WESTERN (CORNIÓN) MASSIF

Vega Huerta Hut   2010m.

Owned by the parks and forestry commission, can be used with
discretion. Door normally open, places for 10, water 25m.
distant, table and benches, old kitchen equipment. Condition of
hut in 1979 was bad, almost unusable. Good campsites. A FEM
hut with 40 places and restaurant services is scheduled to be
built on this important site. At this time it is planned to upgrade
the Camino del Burro trail to jeep road status. Situated on W
side of a broad saddle area dotted with knolls, and below S face
of the Peña Santa de Castilla. Not easy to find in poor visability
The approach from the lower Valdeón, starting at Cordiñañes,
is long, steep and difficult to follow; not recommended. Worse
still from Caín.

13.   Camino del Burro trail. From the Puerto de Panderruedas carpark (1450m.), long but mostly gentle. At E edge of
large parking/camping area a mule trail marked Mirador de
Piedrashita traverses wooded slopes N past latter viewpoint,
and goes in and out of hollows and round ribs on the Valdeón
side of a long grassy ridge, eventually to cross the latter twice
in the vicinity of the Ha. del Frade (1780m.). A steep section
up a ravine follows, Canal del Perra, track disintegrating, to
a col under the Pico del Verde. Now pass to the other (E) side
of the main ridge and follow occasional waymarked stones N
with rough ground to cross another shoulder and so pass under

W side of the Te. de Cotalbin (2193m.). The latter is an excellent viewpoint. So reach the Vega Huerta saddle beyond and arrive directly at hut site ($4\frac{1}{2}$-5 h. from carpark).

14.   From the Vegabaño hut, the usual and best way at present. Follow a good path in woods SE leading to the main tributary of the Rio Dobra. On the other side the same path leads past a fountain and eventually leaves the woods to reach a saddle under pt. 1790m.   Continue N by a track to join the path of R.13 at the Ha. del Frade, then as for latter route ($3\frac{3}{4}$ h. from Vegabaño).

Vega Redonda Hut   1560m.

FEM.   The easiest hut to reach in the Picos de Europa. Pleasant but a bit rough, 20 places, table, benches, fountain and trough nearby. Door normally open in summer. Situated near the head of the Jungumia valley, a few m. from streambed. Herds of cows make camping risky; good flat site about 5 min. up valley from hut on main trail.

15.   From the Enol lakes follow level jeep road S and W to cross a broad saddle (1086m.) and contour to an obvious carpark on R where road starts to descend. Possible to take a car beyond this pt. down to small meadow just before bridge over the dry Redemuña streambed at the Poza del Alemán (7 min. on foot). From here follow deteriorating road L then R to the Vega de la Piedra huts. Circle round sharp L (SE) and follow a beautifully kept path at a moderate angle with decorative waymarks continuously in the SE direction up shallow valley troughs to a small pasture and huts. A similar ascent continues to a little saddle from where a short descent and rocky reascent (note fork R marking start of a major variation to Mirador de Ordiales and Pidal's tomb) lead to the Jungumia valley with hut in view ahead ($1\frac{3}{4}$ h. from carpark).

Marquis de Villaviciosa Hut   1582m.

Owned by the Asturias local authority (Oviedo), mostly used for organised mountain courses. Kitchen, dining room, restaurant service in summer when warden in attendance, running water in hut, 36 places. Inquire at Enol lakes motel if open; keys not otherwise available locally. Situated in the Vega de Ario, giving access to a large number of little known but excellent scrambles and rock climbs.

16. From the Enol/Ercina lakes road terminus carpark below motel, the best route follows paths always SE and fairly clear via the chalets of Ercina, Las Bobias, Redondiella, Las Reblagas, Los Llagos hoyo, Las Compizas, to the Jito col; descend from here in 10 min. to hut (about 3 h. from carpark). The path is not clearly shown on any map.

Central Massif from Peña Santa de Castilla

HUT TO HUT CONNECTIONS

A number of these connections correspond with approaches to main summits. They are often trackless and cross ground which is sometimes steep, loose and very confusing to follow in poor visability.

UBEDA - CABRONES
Horcada Arenera de Abajo   2279m.

17.   From the Ubeda hut descend approach path SW and leave it to traverse round head of the Vega de Urriello, W and NW with a small track in parts, to pass below a group of small towers at the foot of the NE ridge of El Neverón and slant R to reach the ridge at the Corona del Raso (2010m.).   On the far side descend a little to a trench and ascend this to its exit, then work R (NW) across a broad spur into a hollow below the Arenera pass which is soon reached.   Descend a short way NW in a rocky ravine below, then bear sharp L (S) and cross rough ground to a shoulder/saddle under pt. 2324m. on R.   From here go down slabby ground in a curve R (NW) to join the valley system link- ing the Cerredo and Negro hoyos.   Exit from latter keeping L and enter the Cabrones hoyo where hut is found near the S edge (2¼ h.).   I-.   About same time in reverse direction.   Trackless after the Arenera saddle with a few cairns and waymarks.

VERÓNICA - CABRONES
Collada Blanca   2310m.
Horcada Arenizas Baja, or de Caín   2339m.
Horcada Arenizas Alta, or de Don Carlos   2410m.

A problematical connection with two possible outward legs, both with considerable reascents, and using several cols.   R. 18 is also the easiest approach from Verónica biv. to the Cerredo. Grade I/I+.

18.   From Verónica biv. hut go up slabby limestone rib at the back to just below its rounded head which is turned by a traverse

L to reach a broad rock bridge dividing two small snowfields. At the far side turn sharp L to make a slightly descending traverse over honeycomb rock below an outlying spur of P. Tesorero. Continue this more or less horizontal movement for 250m. distance to round a corner R (cairn) where a track and natural traverse ledge takes a slightly descending line above the Sengros hoyo to rise at the far end (snowbeds) and reach the broad Blanca saddle at foot of the Te. Blanca. Running water under L side of ridge rising to latter peak (35 min.).

From Ca. Blanca descend stones and grass into the Trasllambrión hoyo, poor track petering out. Lower down keep R across snow above bed and aim to rise across steep loose rubble on R side to reach a raised rock barrier closing outward end of hoyo at its R side; small saddle (2322m.). Here move R (facing out) for 50m. to above a bank of slabs running below. Descend a shallow crack in these (20m., I/I+) to terraces, then make a descending traverse R (facing out) to quit this upper barrier. Below are long slopes running down to the Jou Grande. Descend these for 200m. keeping slightly R. In bed (c.2075m.) keep R and almost immediately go up R side of an obvious scree fan, past a huge isolated rock, into narrows bearing R and giving access to cwm below the Baja col. After the narrows, steep and loose, trend up L side of cwm then follow bed to col at top. An alternative to this reascent section is to use small track marking original way over col and down to Caín. To join this, do not ascend scree fan; continue in hoyo/valley bed for some distance to its more elevated lip. From here climb scree direct to join track which follows closely below the cliffs of the Coello and Oso, working high up L side of cwm to col at top; not thought to be any quicker or better ($2\frac{1}{2}$-3 h. from Verónica).

On far side of the Baja col traverse horizontally NNW with a faint track to join a slightly better one coming from below. The track rises gradually with snow patches to a steep earthy part (variation below), then crosses a rocky ledge line R, always

A   Bermeja 2606

B   Cerredo 2648

C   Coello 2584

D   Saint–Saud

E   Labrouche (behind)

F   Oso 2571

G   Arenizas Alta col 2410

FROM S

H Arenizas Baja col 2339

J Boada 2513

K Pardida 2572

L Neverón N 2559

M Neverón S 2548

N Arenizas N 2515

P Arenizas S 2502

in the same direction, to reach the Alta col, snow capped to end July (30 min. from Baja col).

Go down NW side direct with a poor track in rocks, then trend R to a steeper middle section also taken direct with loose ribs and boot-worn grooves. Further down, steep scree or a snow slope to end July, axe essential, 35°. Many accidents here. Descend to bed of the Cerredo hoyo, nearly always snow, and follow down its L side through narrows into the Negro hoyo. Exit from latter keeping L and enter the Cabrones hoyo where the Cabrones hut is found near the S edge ($1\frac{1}{4}$ h. from Alta col, $4\frac{1}{2}$-5 h. from Verónica hut. In reverse, $5\frac{1}{2}$ h.).

19. Alternative, over the Rojos col. About the same duration as R. 18, equally arduous with a large sack. From Verónica to foot of N side of Rojos col, as for R. 3. Continue along main path towards Ubeda hut to bottom of step just before the Jou sin Tierra. Leave path and trend L over grass, going downhill until rim of latter hoyo is reached. Follow this round in curve from R to L across a sort of sub division in the great hollow, to its W side and continue over humps and depressions briefly to a stone/grass slope closing entrance to valley mounting to the Arenizas cols. Ascend this steep slope trending R to emerge at a rim. Descend a little to snowbed and follow this to exit L. Ascend broken rocks on L side for a few min. then commence a long rising traverse R across an intermediate rock barrier in the now broader valley, finishing near R side up a short sharp rib then a little gully to an area of limestone pavé, cairn. Cross this L and continue up L side of valley, small track often snow covered, to below the Baja col. Pass a short way under this and soon join previous route some distance before the Alta col.

ALIVA - UBEDA

The best way remains R. 1, 3 across the Ha. de Covarrobres and Ha. Rojos, about $4\frac{1}{2}$ h. A more direct route is recommended by some Spanish authorities, co-inciding with an approach to the

Naranjo de Bulnes. Long and hard with a sack of any weight, not recommended, I+.

Horcada del Vidrio   2252m.
Collada Bonita   2422m.   Also for this col, see note under R. 62.
20.   From Aliva hut follow jeep road uphill to just past the Chalet Real; here the road bends sharp L. On the R take a cart track in grass, working R in a contour round a big loop (spur, 1781m.) to traverse under cliffs above the R. C. A. mine workings. Then the track mounts a scree fan and becomes poor as it enters the Vidrio gully of former and current notorious reputation, now above. Climb this unpleasant gully, partly at 35° on very loose rubble with a rising traverse R over a slab at mid-height (fixed stanchion at top), thereafter improving with an exposed traverse R to exit R round a corner on to a steep grass slope. Ascend slope with deteriorating zags to scree above. A steep rising traverse L with a few cairns, bits of track, leads towards L side of this zone. Go up a little to cairns marking route towards the Vieja; ignore. Now traverse R, first with a riser, over slabby ground towards an obvious saddle formed to L, beyond a group of towers (2281, 2291m.). Thus reach the Ha. del Vidrio by a slightly rising movement all the way ($2\frac{1}{2}$ h.). Most mapping bad hereabouts.

Cross a gentle slope on the other (N) side to pick up a few cairns leading to rockbands round the Infanzon hoyo. Terraces across these lead into a small gorge with a ramp exit on its far side giving access to a scree valley under El Cuchallon (2416m.). A track goes up the valley to slabby steps at the top, giving access to the saddle of Las Colladetas (2290m.). Beyond, a slightly rising traverse over scree leads to steep grass, earth and stones below gap on L side of the prominent finger peak of Ag. de los Martinez. Ascend a few zigzags L to gap of the Ca. Bonita ($1\frac{1}{4}$ h.). Note that broader saddle to R has cliffs on other side. All mapping inconsistent hereabouts.

On the other side an unpleasant rock and rubble funnel with a poor track is taken steeply for 150m. into the Jou Tras el Picu.

INFANZÓN HOYO
from Ha. del Vidrio

CASTIL
2444

2382

CUCHALLÓN
2416

•BONITA
col

OSO
2460

COLLADETAS   MARTINEZ
2451   2422

2290

20

20

Cross steep rough ground N and rise a little to reach the saddle Ca. de la Celada (2246m.) adjoining the impressive S face of the Naranjo (30 min.). Now go down the steep Celada ravine under the Naranjo, poor tracks on its L and R edges, to exit bearing L (W) at the edge of the Vega de Urriello, about 15 min. from hut along a good track (30 min., $4\frac{3}{4}$ h. from Aliva. Most parties should allow at least another hour).

Notes: There are good biv. sites in the Infanzon hoyo. Biv. enclosure near a fountain (Fuente del Mogo) below track across cwm, in bed under SE spur of El Cuchallon, at c. 1900m.

A much less tiring way over ridge in neighbourhood of the Vidrio saddle, ignoring the Aliva departure point and thus avoiding the Vidrio gully, is to cross the Canalona col from the Verónica side, ascend track towards Santa Ana peak for 5 min. to a level shoulder then take a secondary track, generally poor, forking R. It slants L (N) down side of a hoyo, keeping fairly high, crossing several slabby areas and some steep scree to join the SE ridge of To. Navarro just above pt. 2371m., some distance above the Vidrio saddle. Moderate slopes on the other side lead into the Infanzon cwm. By this route from the Verónica biv. hut, 2 h. to shoulder behind pt. 2371m.

VERÓNICA - JERMOSO

Tiro Callejo 2515m.   Tiro Llastriu c. 2550m.

A double col formed across the confusing NNW and NNE prongs of the Llambrión summit ridge. This connection passes close to summit of latter important peak and most parties will make a diversion to visit it. All maps contradict each other as to position of crossing either side of pt. 2621m. - actually on the lower (NNE) side, and place the Te. de las Llastrias (2598m.) generally on the wrong (NNW) ridge. Axe advisable, I+.

21.   From Verónica hut as for R. 18 to the Ca. Blanca (2310m.), 35 min. On the Trasllambrión hoyo side make a descending traverse W under the flanking rocks of ridge below the Blanca peak, over scree. In a few min. descend more steeply over slabby rock and stones and when the angle eases move L to a

large snowfield at foot of Llambrión gl. (15 min.). Cross snow-field, rising a little to reach rocks on far side. Climb a large broken rock spur, first R then L, finishing up a broad rib close to the steep part of the middle gl. tongue. So reach scree and terraces running R below the upper gl. snowfield, all in a fine position under the Llambrión ridge. Follow this ground along-side snow until the rocks peter out, then make a rising traverse R over snow to the obvious Llastriu saddle at end of the Llam-brión ridge; neck of rocks and rubble ($1\frac{1}{2}$ h., $2\frac{1}{4}$-$2\frac{1}{2}$ h.from the Verónica hut).

On the other side descend a track bearing L under steep rocks forming a facet of pt. 2621m., to head of a gully in the NNW ridge running towards the Te. de la Palanca. Descend steep rocks (I+) with waymarks in this gully, on the true L side at first, then near the bed to screes at the bottom. Waymarks lead out across the Jou del Llambrión to the Jermoso approach path only a short way from the hut further R (45 min., 3-$3\frac{1}{2}$ h.from Veró-nica hut. In reverse, $2\frac{1}{2}$-3 h.).

VEGA REDONDA - VEGA HUERTA

Collado de la Mazada   2030m.
Horcada del Alba   2251m.
Horcada de Pozas   2070m.

A see-saw passage along W side of main ridge of the Cornión massif, one of the finest high level rambles in the Picos, I-/I. Axe useful to end July.

22.   From Redonda hut ascend grass to rear to join and follow main path up R side of valley, eventually reaching a fork at top of a grass slope called Llampa Cimera (1830m.), 30 min. Take R branch and go through a stony then narrow grassy trench under the impressive pillar of Porru Bolu. The excellent path works out L then up a long grass slope in easy zags to the Mazada col (45 min.). On the other side a good traverse path winds round spurs below the Te. de Cebolleda; the Prieta spring lies 50m. below path about 15 min. after leaving col. Follow path to top

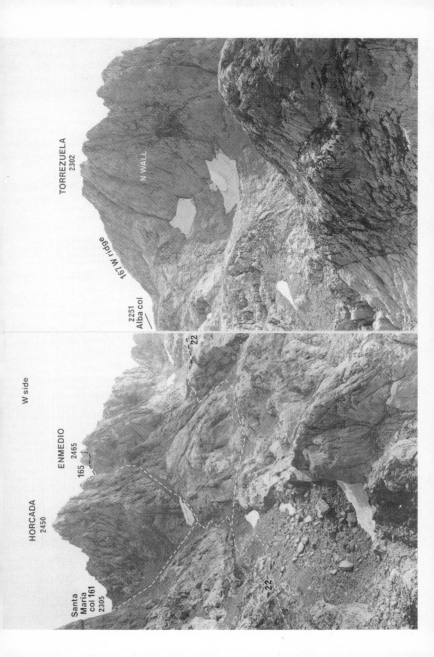

HORCADA
2450

Santa
Maria
col 161
2305

ENMEDIO
2465

165 j

W side

TORREZUELA
2302

167 W ridge

2251
Alba col

N WALL

22

22

of second zigzag below a wide scree opening L, which rises to the Santa Maria col in ridge above; the path continues in this direction. Quit it at this point to traverse R and slightly upwards below a cliff and continue the general direction as before, heading for the large, obvious saddle to L of La Torrezuela (2302m.). There is now only a small broken track in places. So reach the Alba col ($1\frac{1}{4}$ h.). From here go down a steep track in rocks bearing R then L to the upper edge of the Pozas hoyo. Contour round its L (E) side to reach the Pozas col (45 min.). A rough slightly descending traverse follows above the hollow of La Llerona, shortly making a notable reascent to avoid some slabby barriers, towards the striking needle of Ag. del Corpus Christi where a little track descends tortuously below this and soon winds across rock and grass slopes of El Llastral to approach the Vega Huerta saddle; cross this to S side to locate hut and fountain (45 min., 4 h. from Redonda. In reverse, $3\frac{1}{2}$ h.).

Variation: A more roundabout but apparently shorter way round Torrezuela, avoiding the passage of the Alba col. A few m. after passing above the Prieta spring, descend a vague track S to cross a slight shoulder below, then bear L (W) and make a rising traverse SE round the Jou Lluengu, returning R (SW) below the N and W base of La Torrezuela where a descent along a terrace between rockbands leads to a fork. Keep L (S) and rise over scree round the SW spur of Torrezuela and so enter the Pozas hoyo under S side of this mtn. Continue E and SE along bed of hoyo to join previous route and reach the Pozas col.

VEGA REDONDA - VILLAVICIOSA (VEGA DE ARIO)
23. Despite indications of a track on most maps, none agree as regards the best route. This connection is trackless for half its distance, although it crosses easy ground consisting of a series of saddles in parallel ridges running NW to the Enol lakes. Not to be tried in poor visability when route finding

would border on the impossible. At the outset it is best to cross the spur opposite the Redonda hut straightaway to follow up the next valley NE, working up its L fork to between pts. 1822 and 1825 (Cantilumpó). Bear L (E) across a depression behind latter and contour rough slopes into a ravine. Exit under pt. 1968m. (spring) and continue same movement E across the Jous de los Garapozales to ascend and cross a saddle between pts. 1935 and 1957. Descend to a spring at the Vega de la Aliseda where a fairly continuous track is joined. This continues E over the Jorcau la Rasa saddle, under pt. 1812, and at another fork descend L (NE) past Los Cuervos to the grassy plain of the Vega de Ario in the bottom. Move R round base of a spur (1724m.) to old huts then continue L to prominent new building, about 3 h. from Redonda hut.

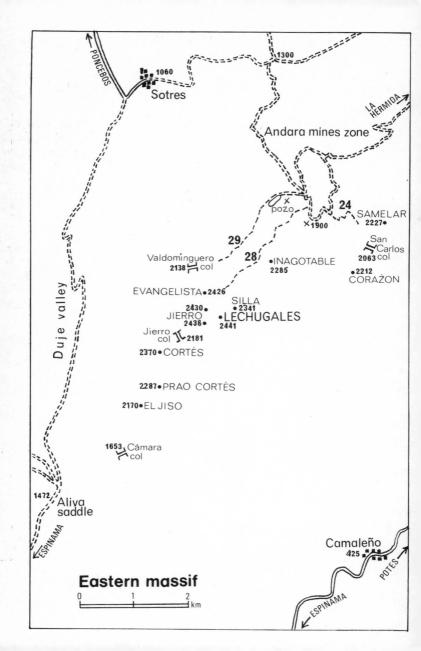

PONCEBOS

1300

1060
Sotres

LA HERMIDA

Andara mines zone

24

pozo
×1900

SAMELAR
2227

San
Carlos
2063 col

29

28

Valdominguero
2138 col

INAGOTABLE
2285

2212
CORAZON

EVANGELISTA 2426

SILLA
2341

Duje valley

2430
JIERRO
2438

LECHUGALES
2441

Jierro
col 2181

2370 CORTÉS

2287 PRAO CORTÉS

2170 EL JISO

1653 Cámara
col

1472
Aliva
saddle

ESPINAMA

Camaleño
425

POTES

Eastern massif

0   1   2
km

ESPINAMA

EASTERN (ANDARA) MASSIF

PICO DE SAMELAR   2227m.

24.   Prominent summit at E side of Andara cirque. Several
short climbs on good rock, III. At sharp bend (c. 1820m.) in
jeep road E of the Providencia mines, a good path leads S then
NE, E and SW in several twists to reach the Co. de San Carlos
in 45 min. The main track continues to latter summit. From
pass follow other ridge to our summit, 30 min., I. First recorded ascent, Saint-Saud, 1890.

COLLADO DE SAN CARLOS   2063m.

25.   Between the Samelar and Sagrado Corazón, ascended on
the Andara cirque side by a good track, R. 24. The other (E)
side is marked by the impressive San Carlos gully, normally
steep snow to end July; in good conditions it offers a direct way
down to Potes with a fairly good but complicated path beyond
foot of gully, I+, $4\frac{1}{2}$ h. in descent.

PICO DEL SAGRADO CORAZÓN   2212m.

26.   Also called Pico de San Carlos. From the San Carlos
col, R. 24, by an excellent track in 30 min. 3m. high statue
on summit. I-. The E ridge sports two or three picturesque
tower/pinnacles.

RASA DEL INAGOTABLE   2285m.

27.   Situated in the SW corner of NE segment of the Andara
cirque. Can be reached from the Sagrado Corazón, R. 24, 26,
along the connecting ridge to W by always keeping below crest
on R (N) side to contour a spur under pt. 2261m. before rejoin-
ing ridge at a double gap. Continue up last steep crest to top,
1 h., I. Or more directly from the Mazarrasa mines as for
R. 28.

INAGOTABLE COL   c. 2230m.

28.   Shallow ridge saddle between summit of same name and
El Castillo (2246m.), latter not marked on most maps. From
Andara jeep road just past the Mazarrasa mines, a good track
goes up under W side of ridge crest which divides the Andara
cirque into SW and NE segments. Above the Castillo de Grajal
(2052m.) this ridge eases and the path splits. Take L branch

in the ridge line to S and continue to saddle by a series of zig-zags, $1\frac{1}{4}$ h. On the other side the track rises a little towards the Rasa (reached in 10 min., see R. 27) before turning back and traversing W below El Castillo towards the main ridge again. It continues SW under ridge by gullies, scree and large blocks to cross a shoulder under P. Arce (2286m.) then descends into a hollow where it ends at the old Evangelista mine (c. 2240m.), 45 min., I-.

PICO DEL EVANGELISTA   2426m.

29.   Summit at junction of Eastern massif main ridge and an important NE branch running to Samelar, R. 24-28. Splendid viewpoint. From the minehead, R. 28, ascend a steep rocky slope and gully to ridge gap L (S) of summit, then easy scram-bling, 30 min., I+ ($2\frac{1}{2}$ h. from Andara jeep road and Mazarrasa mines).

An alternative way, equally direct, takes the mining track SW near the Pozo de Andara lakebed to the Redondal pasture beyond, then up a ravine and over a shoulder to contour a cwm and reach the Co. de Valdominguero (2138m.) in the main ridge of the Eastern massif. A smaller track zags up W side of ridge above to a small col immediately L of the To. de la Infan-ta (2261m.). Ascend grassy rocks along the NW ridge to steep scree mounting to the summit, II-, $2\frac{1}{4}$ h.

PICOS DEL JIERRO   2438m.   2430m.

30.   The name is often applied to the Evangelista summit as well. The N and lower top marks pt. on the Andara massif main ridge where the Lechugales spur is detached E. From the P. del Evangelista, along crest with several short gaps and steps giving slab and gully pitches, exposed and interesting, II, 30 min. First ascent by surveyors in 1865.

TABLA (MORRA) DE LECHUGALES   2441m.

31.   Lettuce Table. Highest pt. of the Andara massif, detach-ed E of main ridge. Superb regional view. The summit is composed of a large rock cube with a tilted top, access to which is by a steep chimney, II; the rest is I. First ascent, Saint-Saud party, 1890.

From the Andara cirque the shortest way is by R. 28, then by a direct ascent to ridge between the Jierro tops and Lech-ugales. Finish up a loose chimney in the ridge line to SE, 3 h. From Evangelista over the Jierro tops (you must go back to pt. 2430m.), R. 29, 30, with same finish, 4 h. See also notes in R. 33, 36 for approaches from Aliva side.

SILLA DE CABALLO 2341m.

32. Double summit on side spur E of Lechugales.

HORCADA DEL JIERRO 2171m. 2181m.

33. Double ridge gap between the Jierro tops and P. Cortés, the main obstacle on traverse between Lechugales and Cortés. In this direction stay on L (S) side of ridge, steep loose slabs with pitches of II/II+; turn a tower on S side to reach the further sharp gap below secondary summit 2270m. of Cortés.

The gap is accessible on NW (Aliva) side by tracks slanting NE (L) from jeep road at Campomayor (1400m.), before a double bend in road, across belts of steep grass and scree into the open Jierro gully. Go up this on strips of grassy rock and exit by L branch of gully, steep and loose, I+, 2 h. from road. This approach gives the most direct way on the Aliva side to Lechugales, II+ above gap, about $3\frac{1}{4}$ h. to summit.

PICO CORTÉS 2370m.

34. Prominent summit marking highest pt. in S part of the main Eastern massif ridge. One of the original trig. stations in this area, reached by surveyors in 1870. Large terraced cliffs of 800m. on S side with several climbs of III/IV and scope for more.

By NE ridge from Ha. del Jierro (R. 33), pitches of II+/III over pinnacled secondary summit 2270m. and down into gap 2230m. Above this a regular ridge over shoulder 2356m. to top, $1\frac{1}{2}$ h. Coming from the Aliva side technical pitches can be avoided by exiting R from the Jierro gully (R. 33) to reach gap 2230m. direct.

The normal route ascends the Aliva (W) flank. This is notoriously steep but technically simple though nowadays marred by severe erosion, making the upper loose rock sections very unpleasant; nevertheless climbed frequently. From the jeep road 500m. distance below the chapel of Ermita de la Santuca de Aliva, various tracks rise steeply over grass to the broad scree opening of the Grajas gully, directly in line with the Prao Cortés above. Zigzag direct to join a track coming from R (Camara pass), then traverse L for some distance to cross a narrow spur and by a short descent enter the Covarones gully. A steep track in scree comes up this gully from below. Climb the gully, getting steeper and looser with big blocks to exit R quite near the top along a ledge line traversing R which reaches saddle 2210m. in main ridge directly above exit from Grajas gully (latter, II+). Follow pleasant ridge with 5 short steps to top, I+, 3 h. from road.

PRAO CORTÉS 2287m.

35. Pyramid summit on main ridge after P. Cortés, easily reached along ridge from latter in 20 min., I. Several rock climbs of IV/V up to 900m. high on buttresses forming craggy S/SE side of mtn. with scope for considerable development. Approach to latter is described under El Jiso below.

EL JISO 2170m.

36. Seen from Aliva (W) side, diminuative looking tower on the craggy ridge descending regularly from P. Cortés to the Cámara pass. In fact, on the other (E/SE) side it forms an imposing rock pillar and centrepiece of great buttressed cliffs extending from Cortés to Cámara and beyond, which are among the highest rockfaces in all the Picos, nearly 800m. at the maximum pt. and giving routes of 1000m. in length. The approach to this area is easy, by crossing the Cámara pass and making a slightly descending traverse over scree under the fairly regular base of cliffs (1 h. to foot of Jiso S pillar), right along to the foot of the big buttresses below the Prao Cortés (1½ h.). Beyond this it is possible to traverse still slightly downwards between rockbands into and across the easy Cortés ravine and so reach the Lechugales ravine which provides a steep scree approach to that summit (by this route from jeep road, 4 h.).

The Jiso has a modern classic rock climb up its prominent S pillar. 600m., V, first done in two stages in 1969. The pillar edge stands above a large wall which is climbed R, on the L edge of a gully cutting it, into a large hollow whose rim is followed L to foot of pillar proper. The route stays mostly on the crest or just L of it. The best descent is to follow the main ridge N into a gap and over an elongated tower to the foot of a smaller square tower (II and bits of III). Below this descend steep scree and loose rock into the Grajas gully (R. 34).

PICOS DE CÁMARA 2050m.

37. Three turreted rock summits between El Jiso and the Cámara pass. Rock climbs of 400m. on E side.

COLLADO DE CÁMARA 1653m.

38. Conspicuous grassy saddle at S end of Eastern massif main ridge. The W side opens directly above the Puertos de Aliva jeep road system, at junctions reached up the Duje valley from Sotres, the Nevandi valley from Espinama, both at the pt. where another road forks W to the Aliva hut. As a pass it has been frequented for a long time by hunters and shepherds but the descent on the Deva (E) side to Camaleño is long and

tedious and of no particular interest to visitors. On the Aliva
side tracks slant up to pass from several pts. on jeep road; a
direct ascent can be made from road below it at the Aliva hut
fork (1476m.), 30 min., I-. For crossing to the other side
and traversing below the SE side cliffs of Jiso-Cortés, ascend
the main ridge for about 100m. distance before going round.

Andara Massif Traverse

This is the most ambitious and worthwhile general mountaineering objective in the Eastern zone. The main ridge is trav-
ersed, normally S to N, from the Cámara pass (R. 38) to the
Valdominguero pass (R. 29). In the first and most serious
section over the Cámara, Jiso and Cortés summits to the Jierro
gap there are pitches of III, thereafter II+ to the Jierro tops
and Lechugales (a diversion); finally scrambling over the Evangelista top and down to the Valdominguero col (8-10 h. including
short halts). The traverse can be continued with little difficulty
over the P. de Valdominguero (2246m.), etc. before descending
to the Andara mines jeep road.

Cabrales East peaks (Naranjo centre left) from Peña Vieja

EASTERN (ANDARA) MASSIF   W side

A   Cueto Tejao   2128

B   Valdominguero   2246

C   Ca. de Valdominguero   2138

D   Infanta   2261

E   Evangelista   2426

F   Jierro   2438

G   Lechugales   2441

H   Ha. del Jierro   2171

J   Jierro gully

K   Cortés   2370

L   Saddle   2210

M   Prao Cortés 2287

N   Covarones gully

O   Grajas gully

P   El Jiso 2170

R   Camara towers 2050

S   Co. de Camara 1653

T   Ha. del Vidrio 2252

U   La Garmona 2291, 2281

V   Aliva/Duje jeep road

Z   Peña Sagra 2046

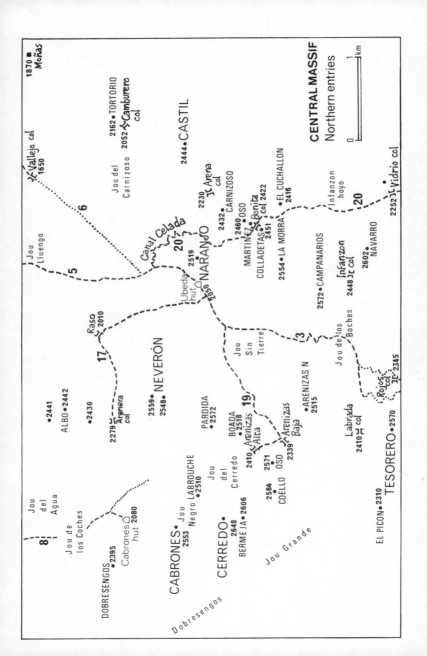

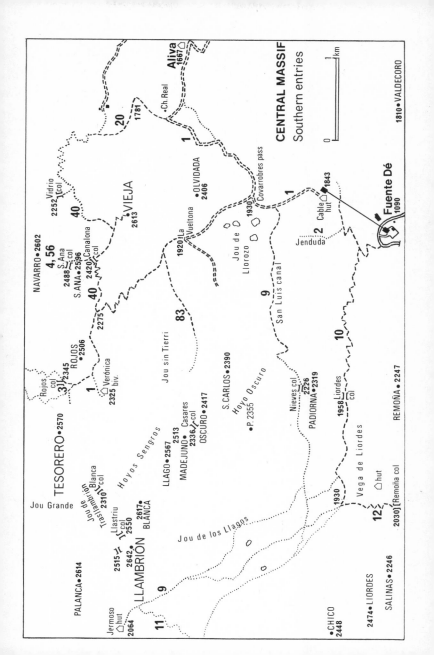

CENTRAL (URRIELES) MASSIF

ALIVA – CABRALES EAST

PICO DE VALDECORO   1810m.

39.   Towering promontory above Deva valley and Espinama.
Easiest access is from top of Fuente Dé cableway, ascending
to and following grassy escarpments with tracks E to pt.1909m.
Here descend S to a saddle and go over next cockcomb SE
(1841m.) with a further descent to another saddle, then a short
rocky ridge to summit, I, $1\frac{1}{4}$ h.   A route of 350m., V, on S face
is reckoned among the first 100 best rock climbs in the Picos.

PEÑA VIEJA   2613m.

Old mountain.   Massive, complicated mtn., easily the most
frequented major summit in the Picos, visited on a fine day in
season by up to 200 persons.   Excellent viewpoint.   First recorded ascent: Saint-Saud party, 9 July, 1890.
    The mtn. deploys a Y shaped ridge.   The stem commences
directly above the Covarrobres pass (jeep road).   From here
the chief landmarks are: initially a cluster of huge pinnacles,
collectively called Tajahierro, also with individual names, then
a notable step/shoulder followed by a regular steep ridge level-
ling off at the summit called Peña Olvidada (2406m.).   Latter is
regarded as a separate top.   Ridge dips beyond then rises progressively at a moderate angle with several short steps as the
S ridge proper to main summit.   The NW branch of the Y descends
to the Canalona col, the NE branch to steep rubble and grass
above the Vidrio gully.   The elongated E/SE flank of the mtn.
overlooking Aliva hut presents cliffs and buttresses over 600m.
high.   A similar but more featureless cliff reaching 400m. in
places extends all along the W/SW (Vueltona) side.   The facet
enclosed by the Y provides the normal route.

40.   <u>North-West Facet</u>.   Loose and slithery at top, otherwise
a good path, I-.   Either from top of Fuente Dé cableway, or
from Aliva hut over the Covarrobres pass, by R.1 to the Canalona junction, marker rock.   Here ascend an equally good path
R, the upper part in easy wide zags over steep scree into a
short gully giving access to the Canalona col (2420m.), 30 min.
Turn R and follow a narrow but good track in debris under L
side of NW ridge, touching crest in places, then over a saddle

PEÑA VIEJA
SW SIDE

S RIDGE

Canal col

NARANJO DE BULNES
FROM SW

and up steep scree on the facet, various tracks, to a zone of broken slabs. Ascend these in loose zigzags with much erosion of path, bearing R at top to summit, 45 min. ($2\frac{1}{2}$ h. from cableway, 3 h. from Aliva hut).

Descent by Vidrio gully to Aliva hut (not recommended in ascent). Go down to saddle under facet. A track forks R from main one. Follow this below flank of NE ridge to lower edge of hoyo under N side of mtn. Keep slightly R, path now vague, a few cairns, and descend a series of bluffs, down to a ravine, exit crossing on your L. After crossing L, traverse R and bear round L to head of screefields (a few cairns) running down below the Ha. del Vidrio, where further down grass and a small track are encountered. Continue down as for R. 20 into Vidrio gully, I/I+ (2 h. from summit to hut).

41. <u>South-East Face Original Route</u>. Effectively the easiest direct way from Aliva hut, but in itself on this face the least direct route of all. Variable on slabs, II+/III, 500m. A. Alonso, J. A. Odriozola, 25 August, 1944.

A large depression opens midway between the summit area and P. Olvidada. At the bottom the R side is marked by a clean cut rib, really the toe of a big buttress further R towards the summit line. From Aliva hut follow jeep road and go round sharp bend L just after Chalet Real; then leave road and climb diagonally over grass and steep scree/blocks to foot of face in 35 min. from hut.

Start in small slabby gullies L of rib. Trend L on broken rock into hollow above. Ascend this bearing L on loose rock and exit L over a short rockband in top L-hand corner to reach an area of slabs and shallow grooves. Ascend these trending L, delicate in places, to near the foot of cliffs high up under Olvidada. Now trend R on similar but slightly steeper ground, above a long, narrow slanting rockband. Steep exit to S ridge at a horizontal spot. Follow ridge, crossing several little gaps,

PEÑA VIEJA NW FACET

AG. DE LA CANALONA

climbing or turning two short steps, and finally along a sharp section to a steep buttress. Turn this R up a ramp and gully to reach a shoulder. Steep scrambling with a gap leads to the summit ridge and top ($3\frac{1}{2}$ h. from Aliva hut).

42.   South-East Face Classic Red Gullies.   So called direct route.   One gully starts at top of the initial hollow crossed L by R. 41.   It is mostly loose and has a number of short steep pitches, III/III+ with bits of IV, 600m.   Ribs can be used on its L and R side.   More commonly used is a gully opening further R, giving similar work with diversions on L side up to a common exit on S ridge not far from the summit step which is turned R as in R. 41 (4 h. from Aliva hut).   A. Alonso, F. Soberón, 31 July, 1945.

43.   South-East Face French Buttress.   Takes the middle area of the first large buttress mass R of the central depression (R. 41, 42).   Starts from gully fan at R base of this mass and works trending L to centre line on buttress.   One of the finest rock climbs of its class in the Picos, generally IV+ with several pitches of V/V+, 650m.   Included in the Rébuffat 100 Best Climbs series of books as an appendix to the Pyrenees.   P. Forn, B. Trouvé, 18 August, 1967.   Other routes on this buttress.

44.   East Spur.   Enormous rock spur in summit line dividing the Aliva wall of the mtn. into two distinct parts.   From near R base, by crest direct, IV, not sustained, variable rock, complicated, 550m.   Two major variations on steep wall to R give better climbing to the spur crest reached at 1/3rd to mid-height, V/V+.

45.   South-West Face Routes.   Above the Vueltona jeep road-head an extensive slope of scree and blocks runs under this face.   The summit cliffs are distinguished by wavy horizontal bands of red and yellow rock.   A direct route just L of summit line gives the Via de los Cantabros, 400m., IV+ with pitches of V, first done in 1978.   Immediately R, the original direct route follows near R edge of a pillar/buttress marking summit line, on excellent rock, 400m., IV with pitches of IV+/V-.   J. M. Albarellos, A. Cianca, J. Rubio, M. Torralbo, 26 December, 1977.   Other routes to L and R of these are easier but on unpleasantly loose rock.   Note: scree is frequently poised just in balance below these cliffs and stonefall is a hazard (even on the road) until the cliffs proper can be reached.

46.   Olvidada Routes.   Generally this summit (=Forgotten Peak) offers continuous technical climbing for the cragsman.   The easiest way off is by the main ridge and R. 41 (III).   Climbs on the Aliva side follow two buttresses, one in summit line, the

other L, and depression flanking them: IV+/V, 400m. Further L is an imposing triangular facet, orientated S, not far from the Covarrobres pass; this gives a first rate climb of 450m., V/V+ with some artificial work. J. Alonso, J.M. San Cristóbal, 27-28 September, 1975.

The Tajahierro pinnacles on lower part of S ridge are just as impressive as the more famous Canalona group further N. The enormous lower frontal one (Ostaicoechea) above the pass gives a 100m. route on its S face by a weakness slanting R to exit up a gully R to reach the inner/rear side (gap) from where a diagonal line R then a direct pitch followed by a short traverse L and final pitch lead to summit, IV+. Abseil descent. P. Udaondo, A. Urones, 9 January, 1966.

The 400m. SE side is noted for several interesting routes, all starting a short distance above jeep road to La Vueltona. R of summit line a complicated zigzag system of ledges and ramps ascends face to emerge L virtually at summit, pitches of III/III+. Various lines avoiding the zags give straighter routes of IV/IV+ & V. At R side of face, before merging into S ridge flank, is a buttress giving one of the most interesting climbs hereabouts, V- (1977). A descent/ascent from/to main ridge at L (N) end of this face is possible on mediocre rock and a bad gully/depression at grade II/III.

COLLADO DE LA CANALONA   2420m.

47.   Between the Vieja and Santa Ana, an important access col provided with an excellent path. See R. 1, 4, 20, 40. It gives its name to a group of pinnacles in the Santa Ana direction which are among the most frequented short climbs in the Picos.

AGUJA DE LA CANALONA   2515m.

Gigantic pinnacle situated on W side of ridge midway between the Canalona col and Santa Ana. Very popular rock climb. A. Alonso, A.M. & J.T. Martinez, J.A. Odriozola, 8 August, **1948.**

48.   East Face. Above gap separating needle from a secondary pt. to its rear, this face is orientated L, towards the parallel main ridge, but at the level of the gap, or rather above it, the route crosses base of the N face (big twin cracks above) to reach it. The normal access to gap is as serious as the final climb itself, being both technical and rather loose with stonefall danger. The rock itself is excellent. An easier access (II), normally used in ascent after climbing the pinnacle, takes the gully below gap which rises parallel to main ridge and exits on

Ag. Bustamante 2380
49

its crest about halfway up the normal route to Santa Ana. 75m.,
III+ with moves of IV-. Scratched.

Below final gully on W side of Canalona pass track (R.1,40)
cross large blocks L (N) and go up a scree fan/gully on R side
of pinnacle base to a short wall on L giving access to a sloping
terrace. Climb wall from R (upper) end (III) and traverse L to
gully below gap. Climb gully with short pitches of III/IV-, quite
a lot of loose material. From gap climb a short wall to a narrow slab band with huge flake rocks above. Traverse L below
these to climb a flake near L end, passing behind its top to reach
further L an open corner/crack (III+). Take this vertical pitch
(IV-) to a ledge. Step L and climb a pinnacle/flake to its top,
then pull up a wall to summit (III+). Abseil blocks and pegs.
1 h. Several harder routes.

AGUJA BUSTAMANTE 2380m.

49. This pinnacle lies below and some distance W of the Canalona one, and is quite conspicuous from trail on W side of the
Canalona col (R.1,40). Reached easily over scree, the normal
way starts from gap to rear, reached from R side, from where
the inner N facet is climbed direct, 40m., IV. A.M. & J.T.
Martinez, 8 August, 1948. Several longer, harder routes.

PICOS DE SANTA ANA 2596m.

Twin triangular summits. The E top on main ridge is the measured pt. It has an uncairned adjoining pt. to W across a little
gap which is slightly higher. The true W summit (2573m., but
hardly believeable) is some distance along ridge in Te. Rojos
direction. It looks higher but from surrounding viewpoints it
appears of equal or lesser height, but not 23m. lower. To cross
from E to W summit proper involves a descent from uncairned
top by gap/gully on N side, followed by a slabby traverse of
some distance into a gap (2558m.), then up a sharp crest of
brittle rock, III-. First ascent: P. Labrouche, 29 July, 1892.

50. East Facet. The normal route, short, popular, loose and
unpleasant, L. Often combined with ascent of P. Vieja (adds 1 h.
to outing). From Canalona col (R.1,40), turn L and go up a good
track to a flat shoulder in a few min. A track goes L up the
facet. Follow it over steep loose rock in zags L and R. Nearly

halfway up by moving further L than necessary a shoulder on main ridge can be reached where exit gully arrives from the Canalona pinnacle, seen splendidly below. Either continue up R side of main ridge on better rock or follow zags sweeping R and back L in middle of facet, narrowing at top and by keeping L finally go up a groove R and just under ridge crest to cairned summit (40 min. from Canalona col).

51. <u>West/North-West Face of W Peak</u>. Several climbs of 150m. on sound rock, III+ to IV+.

52. <u>West Ridge of W Peak</u>. From gap 2506m. in ridge running to Te. Rojos, pleasant scramble of II+.

53. <u>Rojos - Santa Ana Ridge</u>. A long scramble, finishing by R. 52. Initial descent from Te. Rojos over slabby bluffs for 125m. to saddle 2384m. (II), then keeping to L side of ridge and turning by a low traverse well below crest a steep narrow section, to reascend and rejoin crest which is followed over pt.2515 into gap 2506m. at foot of R. 52. 3 h., II+.

TORRE DE LOS HORCADOS ROJOS 2506m.

One of the most frequented rock climbing sites in the Picos, access being short and simple. The blood red S wall dominates background on walk from cableway to the Rojos col, R. 1, 3. As a summit viewpoint it is superior to Santa Ana.

54. <u>North-West Facet</u>. Steep and loose in parts due to erosion from the passage of feet, I-. From the Rojos col go up obvious zigzag trail to rocky bits in slippery grooves, later working a little R before resuming a direct ascent to a forepeak. Cross a little gap to main summit (20 min. from col, $2\frac{1}{4}$-$2\frac{1}{2}$ h. from the cableway, 3 h. from Aliva hut, 1 h. from Verónica hut).

55. <u>South Wall</u>. The wall is directly opposite the Verónica hut and all routes start a few min. above the Rojos col trail. Just L of summit line the wall is cut vertically at a wedge of rock by a huge chimney/gully. This is joined nearly halfway up from the L by an obvious weakness. The original route takes the L-hand weakness and continues up the main chimney/gully, 300m., IV+ with a pitch of V. Scratched. A. Landa, J.M. Régil, P. Udaondo, 27 September, 1958. Direct start (harder than the

SANTA ANA W RIDGE

W 2573
2558 E 2596
152
2515
Risco del Huso
53
2506
51
WNW face

Canalona
48
col
40
Busta-mante
49

2384

BLANCA normal route

96
95
NNE RIDGE

96

Sengros bridge

from pt. 2383

L-hand way) by lower chimney/gully, IV+ (1962). Further L is
the Via Juanin, taking mostly L side of a narrow pillar/rib situated L of a prominent gully; some of the rock needs care, 300m.,
IV+. J. C. Alonso, J. M. Bustillo, 3 October, 1975. Several
other hard routes have been made of this impressive wall, and
there is scope for more. Convenient cave biv. site at wall foot.

COLLADO DE SANTA ANA   2488m.

56.   Between P. de Santa Ana and To. Navarro, topographic-
ally an important pass but probably not crossed often. Sometimes recommended as an alternative to the Rojos col, via the
Canalona col, but the detour and effort are considerable. Reached easily on E side from the Canalona col by a rising traverse
under Santa Ana, R. 50. After the flat shoulder continue in same
line normally across a small snowfield to the broad saddle, 30
min. from Canalona col, I-. The other side is a long, rough,
steep but regular rubble slope down to the Rojos col N side path
near the Boches hoyo, R. 3.

TIROS NAVARRO   2602m.

57.   Remote and serious mtn. with 3 summits, N highest. Its
S ridge from Co. Santa Ana is V. Circuitous and tedious normal
way crosses Santa Ana pass and descends below W face to reascend and reach the Infanzon saddle (2488m.) at foot of NW
ridge; this is taken over a forepeak (2601m.) to N summit, I.

HORCADA DEL VIDRIO   2252m.

58.   Saddle at foot of long E ridge of To. Navarro, giving best
access to the Infanzon cwm and hoyo on N side of this ridge.
See R. 20.

LOS CAMPANARIOS   2572m.

59.   Multiple summits of similar height along main ridge towards the Naranjo. No special interest.

LA MORRA   2554m.

60.   Important ridge junction at S intersection containing the
Jou Tras el Picu. The peak has a few routes of general mountaineering interest. Rarely climbed.

TORRE DE LAS COLLADETAS   2451m.

61.   This peak introduces the first of a series of striking saw
tooth summits and towers round the Jou Tras el Picu, mostly,

and unusually for the region, characterised by poor rock. The normal route takes a gully out of Jou at R side of summit wall, to small saddle, then up short SW ridge, turning a step R near top, I+ (2½ h. from Ubeda). Saddle can be reached with less effort from the Infanzon cwm side.

COLLADA BONITA 2422m.

62. Between Te. de las Colladetas and Ag. de los Martinez; a notable ridge gap used by climbers crossing the Jou Tras el Picu to reach the Naranjo. See R. 20. The height is almost certainly mistaken and should be assigned to the adjoining Martinez pinnacle. Probable height, 2350m.

AGUJA DE LOS MARTINEZ (RISCO VICTOR) 2422m.

63. See note about height in R. 62 above. Tooth-like pinnacle first climbed by Martinez and Rivera in 1950. From the Jou Tras el Picu a slabby wall (II+) is climbed to saddle in ridge under NE side. Move round to a big groove in E side and climb this on bad rock to sharp summit (III+). The W face is similarly friable.

TORRE DEL OSO 2460m.

64. Height suspect, probably 2480m. or more. Huge rounded tower with a variety of serious routes, most of them on doubtful rock. The easiest is reckoned to be a gully in NW face, rising from head of a big scree fan above the Jou Tras el Picu. After an entry pitch of IV-, easier climbing with some loose rock leads in 120m. to summit. A better route takes the N ridge on sound rock from col 2350m., III+. Both about 3 h. from Ubeda hut.

TORRE DEL CARNIZOSO 2432m.

65. Another impressive tower difficult of access on all sides.

PEÑA CASTIL 2444m.

66. Last important summit at N end of the Cabrales East main ridge, first climbed by surveyors in 1865. The NNW side normal route can be followed from the Terenosa hut, R. 6, by paths S to the Moñas pasture (1870m.) and over a wide saddle further S to traverse SE flank of the Cabezo Tortorio (2162m.) to the Ha. de de Camburero (2052m.). From this pass traverse horizontally W and turn up a long grass and rock slope to reach summit at top, about 4½ h., I.

CUCHALLON DE VILLASOBRADA 2416m.

67.   Fine rock peak rising across the Colladetas saddle (R. 20)
and opposite Te. of this name on main ridge (R. 61).   Largely
undeveloped with a number of possibilities for new routes.   The
easiest way is a gully in NE side.

NARANJO DE BULNES 2519m.

Usually translated as Orange Tree in English literature but actually a reference to prominent orange streaks on the NE face.
It rises as a cornerstone from N edge of the Jou Tras el Picu
and its opposite W and N sides present immense walls above
the Vega de Urriello (Ubeda hut) and Celada gully.   The most
famous peak in the Picos and in all Spain; see historical notes
in Introductory section of guide.   There are at least 20 indep-
endent major route lines on the various walls of this great limestone block, and as many variations again.   The rock is generally excellent and very rough, but patches of poor rock occur
on some climbs.   The smooth, monolithic W/SW face above the
Ubeda face attains a height of 400m., though frequently exagger-
ated to 500m. or more.   It merges L into a huge spur whose
crest faces N and descends to a broad toe marking entrance to
the Celada (=Hidden) gully.   The N spur rises 500m. and climbs
hereabouts are 600m. long.   Round this corner and towering
above as a flank of the gully is the NE face, inclined to E at the
upper L edge; it is noted for a broken undercliff surmounted by
two terrace areas and altogether has an average height of 350m.
At the top of the Celada gully and E face leads round to the S,
the shortest side of all, about 100m. high to the rim of a hollow
called the Amphitheatre, itself giving another 75m. to the summit ridge.   The summit ridge, above all the cliff areas, runs
W-E.   The latter lower end marks the top of the E/NE face.
   First ascent: Pedro Pidal, Gregorio Pérez, 5 August, 1904.
First solo and 2nd ascent: Gustav Schulze, 1 October, 1906.
By a woman: Maria Pérez with A. Martinez, 31 July, 1935.
By a British party: T. J. Fowle, F. Green, F. Watson with
A. Martinez, July, 1950.   In winter: A. Landa, P. Udaondo,
8 March, 1956.   Climbed about 200 times up to 1955, then much
more frequently.

South Face.   This short side of the mtn. offers the easiest
routes to the summit.   All have good stances, belays and excellent rock.   From the Ubeda hut approach by steep loose tracks
up the Celada gully to saddle at edge of the Jou Tras el Picu,
as for R. 20, $1\frac{1}{4}$ h.   Round the corner the face rises from R to
L.   A little ramp in broken rocks under the wall passes a gully
entrance with corrugated rock on its L and a large yellow roof
higher up and R (start of Nani Route, V).   A few m. higher it
levels out momentarily below a corner/crack marking a

discontinuous weakness in wall up to prominent chimney/corner
in R side of face.   After another 20m. along ramp it is possible
to scramble upwards trending L to base of wall again 40m. distance from level place.   Directly above is a horizontal roof with
a terrace extending L at same level.   At same pt. a huge flake
crack forms a bracket slab in upper part of wall below the Amphitheatre.   At wall base a memorial plaque, and somewhat L an
opening to the largest of several small gullies hereabouts. About
15m. further L along wall base is an alcove with a triangular
yellow roof directly above it.

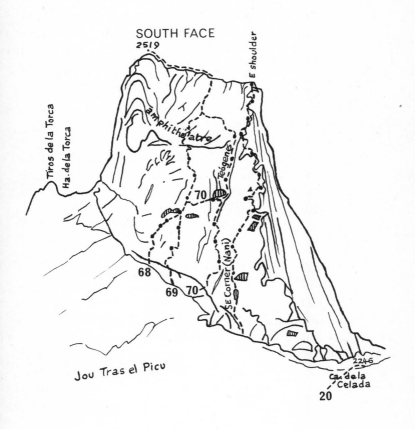

SOUTH FACE
2519

E shoulder

Tiros de la Torca
Ha. de la Torca

amphitheatre

Teógenes

70

68
69 70

SE Corner (Nani)

Jou Tras el Picu

2246
Ca. de la
Celada

20

68.   Original (Victor) Route.   Now the least practised way.
Pitches of IV, one of IV+, 100m.   V. Carrión with V. Martinez,
18 August, 1924.   Start in the alcove and climb trending L into
niche (15m., IV).   Exit R up cracked wall to stance below triangular overhang (10m., IV+).   Make an exposed rising traverse
R to large terrace (15m., IV).   Climb wall cracks just L of edge
of huge bracket slab/flake above, to stance on R halfway up
(20m., III, III+).   Continue in same manner (20m., III) to stance
on R.   Climb a short wall L of corner then make a diagonal
movement L across steep, exposed corrugated slab, the Organ
Pipes, to stance at lower edge of Amphitheatre (15m., IV).
Move a little L then go up back of Amphitheatre roughly in the
centre and finish up cracks/grooves (II, III-) to summit ridge
which is followed L to top. $1\frac{1}{4}$ h. for wall, 30 min. to summit,
about $3\frac{1}{2}$ h. from Ubeda hut.

69.   Direct (Martinez) Route.   Slightly harder at the bottom
but easier overall than Original Route.   110m.   A. & J.T.
Martinez with 6 clients, 13 August, 1944.   Start just L of the
memorial plaque, in line with big terrace at L side of horizontal
roof.   Climb wall L of and parallel with 3 deep cave cracks
(15m., IV, V-), stance.   Traverse 5m. R and take a crack to
stance in niche (25m., IV).   Continue straight up cracked wall
(15m., IV-) to big terrace where R. 68 is joined and followed.
Allow 2 h. from wall foot to summit; about $3\frac{1}{2}$ h. from Ubeda hut.

70.   Paso Horizontal.   Equally frequented as the Direct, this
exposed traverse goes out from the R-hand side chimney/corner
route (V) to join previous routes at stance halfway up the flake
crack.   Generally III+ with bits of IV and a short stretch of
V-, 160m.   (Schulze abseiled down this chimney/corner on the
occasion of 2nd ascent of mtn.).   M. Martinez, solo, 8 August,
1928.   Start from level place on ramp just before corner/crack.
Climb steep rock trending R into a chimney and follow this to
stance 10m. higher (IV-).   Leave chimney and on L climb a

WEST FACE
2519

Tiros de la Torca

A

C

A B

A

BIV.

D

A

L
B
C

2100 contour

72
A. Rabada-Navarro
B. Direct
C. Murciana
D. escape route (IV)

grooved wall trending L to reach gully above, stance (III+).
Take gully to stance below small overhang (IV). Move up turning bulge L (V-) and continue for a few m. to stance below huge bulge on L wall. Traverse L under this and continue by a descending traverse under smooth rock to reascend at far end using a short crack and finish on stance halfway up flake crack, R. 68 (35m., IV). Allow $2\frac{1}{2}$ h. from wall foot to summit.

71. East/North-East Face. The start of climbs on this side, overlooking the Celada gully, is normally reached at large terrace near gully head. At this pt. the sub wall below the face is mostly lower down. The original Pidal route takes a lower weakness in a slightly rising line from the large terrace, over steep slabs to a small screefield adjoining N ridge above its initial step (IV+/V-, rarely used today). Above the screefield is a big chimney/crack system in R side of face. This gives 10 pitches for about 280m., mostly IV, with two of V- and a crux at the 3rd of V. The last 5 pitches are only III or II. Schulze reached the chimney system by climbing wall directly above large terrace, and just L of a Y mass of rock, crossing top of latter R to reach the large upper terrace line (pitches of IV). This leads R into chimney at foot of crux pitch. Other routes on this wall are harder, notably the Cepeda which continues directly above Y mass of rock to enter a crack system further L and much higher up (V); and the Martinez-Somoano route (350m., VI-), one of the best on the mtn., following a weakness further L to be joined by the Cepeda near the top.

Routes on the lower part of the N ridge spur, starting near entrance to Celada gully, generally have pitches of V. All converge at shoulder below the unclimbed upper edge dividing the NE and W sides of the mtn. These climbs therefore finish up the entire length of the Pidal chimney system, altogether giving a route length of 550/600m. The Régil Variant (IV+) coming up the hut flank of the lower spur is the most direct and popular method of doing the Pidal chimney today.

72. West Face. This wall is the showpiece of the Naranjo. The original route remains one of the finest rock climbs of its class anywhere in Western Europe. VI-, A1/2, length nearly 750m. It finishes up the top part of the N spur (the lower part above the halfway shoulder being unclimbed). See diagram. E. Navarro, A. Rabadá, 21 August, 1962. The Direct Route (see notes in Introductory matter to guide) is largely artificial and ranks as VI, A3, 400m. The similar Murciana route was done in 1978 and follows a parallel line L of the Direct. The most recent new climb on this face lies on the R (SW) side, the Leiva route (1979), V, A1/2.

LIORDES – LLAMBRIÓN GROUP

PẼNA REMOÑA   2247m.

73.   Picturesque triple tower dominating W side view from Fuente Dé. Climbed by Saint-Saud in 1892. W tower is highest. As for R. 10 to Co. de Liordes (1958m.). Leave trail and steer S over grass, scree and finally steep rocks to R-hand summit, I ($3\frac{3}{4}$ h.). A route of 900m. with pitches of V+ was made on the E side spur, L of ravine below E tower, in 1969.

TORRE DE SALINAS   2446m.

Celebrated as the first important summit in the Picos to have a recorded ascent: Casiano de Prado and party, 1853. Only in recent times has it revealed a number of good rock climbs. The forestry hut (1900m.) marked on most maps at S edge of the Vega de Liordes, R. 10,12, is a useful base.

74.   <u>East-South-East Ridge</u>. Normal route, I+. From Fuente Dé by R. 10 to fork in trail before Padiorna saddle. Bear L and take next fork L, rising S past forestry hut and zigzagging to the Co. de Remoña (2030m.), 4 h. Or from road above S. Marina to Remoña pass by R. 12, $2\frac{1}{4}$ h. From pass climb steep ridge on broken slabs, generally turning obstacles L and with traces of a path, to small shoulder, followed by a short scramble to top, 45 min. from pass.

75.   <u>North Buttress</u>. Well defined rock mass about 300m. high under summit area. Its facets give climbs on good rock, grades IV+ to V+.

TORRE DEL HOYO DE LIORDES   2474m.

76.   Complicated mtn. with multiple tops and numerous short technical climbs on good rock. Easiest route at R end of NNW face under main summit, II+.

TORRE DEL HOYO CHICO   2448m.

77.   Grave altitude error. It is much lower than Te. Liordes and Friero, probably only 2360m. Rarely climbed (I), it has a fine little gendarme N ridge, 300m., IV, with crux of VI-.

TORRE DEL FRIERO   NW. 2445m.   SE. 2416m.

Magnificent double tower at NW end of Liordes group, directly overlooking Posada de Valdeón. The N side falls into the Asotin ravine (R. 11) and is cleaved by the longest gullies and ribs used as climbs in the Picos.

78.   East Side Ramp and North-East Ridge Summit Gullies.

Normal route, I. Can be reached from Posada/Cordinañes up the very steep Asotin ravine, small track, $3\frac{1}{2}$ h. to foot of ramp. From Jermoso hut by reversing R. 9 to cross rocky hillocks and depressions at bottom of Jou de los Llagos, then by scree cwm exit from Asotin ravine towards the Ca. de Chavida (2122m.), $1\frac{3}{4}$ h. Or from forestry hut on the Vega de Liordes by a track into bottom of Jou, as above, $1\frac{3}{4}$ h. Near top of cwm under Chavida pass, a rock and scree ramp, wide at bottom, narrow at top, slants R under summit cliffs to a shoulder on NE ridge. On R (N) side of crest ascend loose gullies to a fore-peak then main summit, 1 h. from upper cwm.

79.   North Face. Well seen from Jermoso hut. Has a splendid central gully which may hold snow throughout season. Frequently mixed difficulties and some objective danger, 900m., IV, first climbed in 1977. Rib to its R gives a serious open route of 1000m., IV+ (1975), while big gully further R is similarly long at grade III (1978). Other flanks of both summits give routes up to 300m., gnereally IV or harder.

PICO DE LA PADIORNA   2319m.

80.   Promontory of easy access on N side and presenting quite amenable cliffs on S side, latter seen from Fuente Dé. Popular viewpoint. From top of cableway by R. 9 to Ca. de las Nieves, then up a short grass and rock slope in 10 min., I- ($1\frac{3}{4}$ h.). Rock climbs of 300m. on S face, adjoining Liordes col, R. 10.

COLLADINA DE LAS NIEVES   2226m.

81.   Between La Padiorna and pt. 2241m., important pass with small track on both sides, see R. 9.

POINT 2355m.

82.   Worthy little unnamed summit, good training walk, fine
view of Llambrión group. From top of cableway by R. 9 to
ravine entrance of Hoyo Oscuro. Do not continue up cairned
spur to L. Ascend R side of ravine bed and exit R to ascend
broad rock platforms sharp R for 50m. to a level spot. Summit
is at back of hoyo, slightly L. Traverse R side horizontally,
vague track, to grassy spur at centre rear of hoyo. Go up this
to rounded shoulder. Traverse R into upper scree hollow and
mount steep grassy strips beside a rib L to small col 2290m.
at foot of N ridge. Turn first small towers easily R on shattered rock then follow crest or R side to top, I- (2 h.).

PICO SAN CARLOS 2390m.

83.   Tail end of main Llambrión ridge, has undistinguished
profile with huge block called Torre de Altaiz (2290m.) as a
supporting buttress extending towards the Vueltona jeep road
head.   Numerous short technical climbs.   Note, there is no
advantage taking continuation jeep road to old mine workings
on the San Luis canal side, R. 9.   Good training walk/scramble.
From top of cableway follow R. 1 to Vueltona bend and go up the
first 100m. of path towards the Canalona junction, to where
path nears bed on L at a narrow scree outflow (7 min.).   Leave
path, traverse blocks L, cross bed and in 50m. pick up a nice
track going along L (S) side of Jou Sin Tierri and under all the
N side cliffs of Altaiz and San Carlos, higher up working over
rocks while still a track, to just past level of the Ha. Verde.
Now quit track and ascend scree and blocks trending L to latter
col at foot of NW ridge of San Carlos.   Go up this with interest
and some exposure, turning short obstacles L and R to top,
II- (1¾ h.).

HORCADA VERDE 2264m.

84.   Between P. San Carlos and Te. del Hoyo Oscuro, an access
to these peaks. The Hoyo Oscuro (S) side, R. 82, is a long
scree and rock slope, much more tedious than N side approach
by R. 83.

TORRE DEL HOYO OSCURO 2417m.

85.   Regular pyramid with fine rockfaces on the rarely visited
Hoyo Oscuro (S) and more frequented Jou Sin Tierri (N) sides.
Probably climbed by Saint-Saud in 1890. From top of cableway
follow R. 83 past pt. for Ha. Verde and ascend last traces of
path in rocks and scree under N face of mtn. to large hummocky
terraces now running below all peaks towards the To. Llago and

96

Ca. Blanca. The first col above is the Ha. de Casares (2336m.), reached easily up a short rubble slope with small track, $1\frac{3}{4}$ h. Above, climb the NW ridge along slabby crest to a step turned R. Rejoin crest at a section with 4 small pinnacles, turned mainly on L side, to finish up broken crest to summit, II (30 min., $2\frac{1}{4}$ h. from cableway).

86. <u>North Facet</u>. 200m., III+. <u>North-East Facet</u>. 200m., IV+. Several possible lines on each.

HORCADA DE CASARES   2336m.

87.   Between Te. del Hoyo Oscuro and P. Madejuno, important ridge access and crossing pt. for climbers. On NE side, from cableway by R. 83, 85, $1\frac{3}{4}$ h. From Ca. Blanca, R. 18, by descending traverse over slopes under NE wall of To. Llago, round edge of the Jous Sengros, to cross more or less horizontally along rocky terraces below Madejuno to adjoining col, traces of path, snow patches to late season, I-, $1\frac{1}{4}$ h. Or from the Verónica biv. hut, working S and traversing steep slabby slopes into bed of Jou Sin Tierri, then up narrow scree slope SW under Madejuno to terraces below col, 1 h. The Hoyo del Sedo (S) side is a long scree and rock slope, bits of track, running down SW to join R. 9 at the Sedo de la Padiorna. In ascent on this side, $1\frac{1}{4}$ h.

PICO MADEJUNO   2513m.

Distinctive elongated turret with one of the finest short normal routes in the Picos, also with numerous technical climbs, all quite feasible from top of cableway for N side routes, or from Verónica hut by R. 87.

88.   <u>East-North-East Facet</u>. A minor classic, 100m., II/II+ with a pitch of III+. From terraces directly below Casares col, R. 83, 85, ascend broken rock diagonally R in a slight depression normally containing a snow patch, below first step on main ridge marked by the knobbly Tos. de Casares, and exit R to a screeband running back L below facet towards main ridge, 20 min. Start about 40m. R of main ridge and climb a shallow gully/groove weakness slanting R for a rope length. This goes into a vague continuation gully and up to a steep corner pitch taken direct (III+, abseil peg at top). Gully line now trends L; take a short pitch direct, the next on R side, finishing up a wall with landing on slab band forming ridge crest. Climb this in

LLAMBRIÓN GROUP NE side

A B C D E F G H J

Jous Sengros

Ca.●
Blanca

A	Madejuno 2513	F	Llastriu col 2550
B	Llago 2567	G	Llastrias 2598
C	Blanca 2617	H	Hoyo Grande 2550
D	Tirso 2641	J	Palanca 2614
E	Llambrión 2642		

centre to narrow summit ridge and top, 1 h. ($2\frac{1}{4}$-$2\frac{1}{2}$ h. from cableway, rather less from Verónica hut).

89. <u>North Face</u>. This is cut diagonally L to R by a steep ramp. Routes start from lower end of this feature and go up wall in the summit line, several ways, 120m., III to IV. Possibilities for new routes.

90. <u>South Face</u>. Accessible across the Ha. de Casares with only a short descent but over very steep loose scree. Original route direct, 200m., IV+.

TIRO LLAGO 2567m.

Double turret, altogether evident on NE side, much less so on SW side where cliffs mostly attain a modest height. Often climbed in combination with Te. Blanca, easily approached from the cableway, while technical climbs can be started from Verónica biv. hut to save time. First ascent, Saint-Saud party, 1891.

91. <u>North Side Right-Hand Gully and Groove</u>. The normal route, 75m., II-. Most conveniently approached after descending ESE ridge of Te. Blanca and continuing along terrace system slightly downwards on L side of main ridge to pinnacled foot of NW ridge (gap) from where gully can be entered some distance above its entrance by a descending traverse L. Alternatively, same pt. can be reached avoiding Blanca peak, from Ca. Blanca, R. 18, by climbing the Blanca normal route, R. 95, until upper snowfield can be crossed by a rising traverse L to join terrace

LLAMBRIÓN GROUP S cwm

A	Peña Santa de Castilla, behind	F	Tirso 2641
B	Minas de Carbon, S pillar	G	Sin Nombre 2635
C	Minas de Carbon 2595	H	Blanca 2617
D	Casiano de Prado 2622	J	Pt. 2356
E	Llambrión 2642	K	Hoyo de Los Llagos

system under this side of Blanca-Llago ridge. It is not recommended that gully is approached directly from below, in a big snow couloir reached by descending SE from Ca. Blanca en route by the terrace traverse described in R. 87.

At foot of steep NW ridge of mtn. is a narrow gap. From scree a few m. below it traverse outwards L and slightly downwards over broken spikey rocks and enter hidden gully round a corner further L, variable, 30m. distance, I+. Climb loose bed for a pitch to about 20m. below gap at top. A groove system cuts L wall. Take groove on slabby rock following an obvious stepped weakness (II-) to small sloping ledges under short summit wall. Trend R up corner to summit ridge and reach top in a few m., 30 min. from NW ridge gap, $1\frac{1}{2}$ h. from Verónica hut.

92. **North-East Walls.** Routes on shorter true summit tower are 100m., IV+ or harder. The longest climbs are located on bigger face to L, below lower SE tower. Gully between the two towers, mixed climbing with some loose rock, III+. Edge immediately L of latter, IV/V. Outer L edge of this tower, forming an E buttress or spur, gives 200m. at V.

93. **South-West Face.** Remote access, direct route, 250m., V-.

94. **Madejuno-Llago Main Ridge Traverse.** Excellent mountaineering route, in this direction mostly III with short pitches of IV, and short abseils. Combined with R. 101, it ranks as one of the best expeditions of its class in the Picos.

TORRE BLANCA   2617m.

In itself not an important summit but one of the most frequented better viewpoints in the Picos.   It is really the outer E bastion of the immediate Llambrión group.

95.   <u>North-North-East Ridge</u>.   The usual route, very popular, I, axe useful.   From Verónica hut by R. 18 to Ca. Blanca.   Now go up to foot of ridge and turn it L to follow rocks and grass on its L side, on or near crest, to below an initial big step.   Make a rising traverse L to edge of snowfield, or contour over rocks to its immediate R.   Work up nearly to top of snowfield where on the R a narrow gritty gully cuts steeply R to NNE ridge shoulder above its intermediate steps.   From shoulder ascend upper ridge over ledged rocks and bits of track directly to the summit, $1\frac{1}{4}$ h. from Verónica hut.   Ridge direct, probably IV.

96.   <u>East-South-East Ridge</u>.   Normally used in descent to make a little round, or for approaching the Llago.   Short, on smooth slabs with good friction, I+.   From summit descend broad ridge line steepening into slabs which are followed down on L side of crest with one smooth zigzag movement of 10m.   At the bottom keep L of crest along broad terraces to continue towards the Llago (15 min.).   Below is a large slabby rib going down to the huge rock bridge dividing the Jous Sengros.   This can be followed as a variation back to the Verónica hut (recommended).

<u>Other Routes</u>.   Numerous climbs of 200m. have been made on S and NW walls of mtn.

TORRE SIN NOMBRE   2635m.

97.   Minor incident on impressive ridge running from the Te. Blanca to Llambrión, barely discernible from below. See R. 101.

TIRO TIRSO   2641m.

Notable ridge incident just before last uplift to the Llambrión. Its normal route, like Madejuno, is a minor classic.   Easily climbed in same day with Llambrión.   First ascent: G. Schulze, 1906.

98.   <u>West-North-West Ridge</u>.   Fine mini rock climb, 100m., II, sustained and exposed.   The ridge juts off line from main

ridge so that its toe descends below gap adjoining its base.
From Verónica hut by R. 18 to Ca. Blanca and R. 21 to terraces
at foot of upper Llambrión gl. Ascend short gl. snowfield direct to foot of ridge and go up towards main ridge gap, 2 h.
About 10m. below gap step L on to rounded ridge and climb its
slabby rock keeping first slightly R on short steps, then L, up
to a shoulder platform at 2/3rds height. Step down and move
L into shallow gully and ledge system rising parallel with crest
line, and go up to ledges and short walls at top of this system.
Take upper broken wall trending L to crest which is followed
for a few m. to top (30 min.).

99.   <u>South Face Routes</u>. Several lines, all about 300m., III+
V+.

TORRE DEL LLAMBRIÓN   2642m.

As a topographical summit, ranks among the most important
elevations in the Picos, as well as being 2nd highest pt. in the
range. However its rock climbing interest is concentrated in
big spurs running off S and W. Good viewpoint. The actual
summit is not easily identified from below, and this was the
cause of early confusion over its exact location. It can be
perfectly appreciated from P. Tesorero. First ascent: Casiano
de Prado, J. Boquerin, 12 August, 1856. 2nd was not until
1892, by Saint-Saud party.

100.   <u>Normal Routes</u>. Start from pts. along R. 18, 21, quite
straightforward, I+, axe useful. From Verónica hut proceed
to terraces along base of upper Llambrion gl. Ascend gl. snowfield trending R to highest snow tongue under summit wall, with
summit line slightly L. Bergschrund possible, transition from
snow to rock delicate. Go up a few m. into steep gritty hollow
whose rear wall is cut by various gullies. Climb hollow trending R into a narrow yellow-red gully going up to ridge at last
level place R (N) of summit. Climb gully with bridging tactics
to short terminal wall and landing on knife edge (I+, fairly
sustained). Go up R side of crest to top in 30m. ($2\frac{1}{4}$-$2\frac{1}{2}$ h. from
Verónica hut).

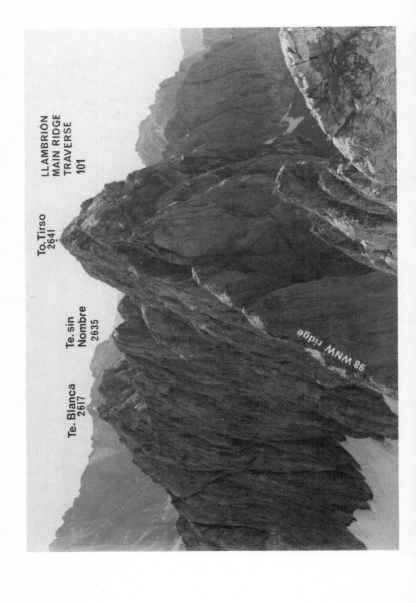

Te. Blanca
2617

Te. sin
Nombre
2635

To. Tirso
2641

LLAMBRIÓN
MAIN RIDGE
TRAVERSE
101

98 WNW ridge

From Jermoso hut, by reversing R. 21 nearly to Llastriu saddle, go up the NE ridge facet over steep broken rock to a track below crest on R side, and along to a short sharp gap. Climb out of this by a broken wall R (I+) and continue on R side then up to sharp crest before last riser where Verónica side chimney emerges (2 h. from Jermoso hut).

101. <u>Blanca-Llambrión Main Ridge Traverse</u>. Classic expedition, exposed, with fine situations, not serious for experienced climbers, III/III+. First recorded traverse, 1950. From Blanca summit descend exposed rounded crest to a level section, dropping into a gap (III). Climb out trending R and follow slabby crest in short steps to top of Te. Sin Nombre (II). Either climb (III+) or abseil into V gap, then traverse a little tower to another small gap (III). Continue near steep crest to top of To. Tirso and descend by R. 98 to deep gap. In ridge wall ahead climb a chimney R (III+) to gap behind first tower. Traverse next small tower (III) or turn it R using a ledge line to rejoin crest by a short chimney R (II+). Continue up crest to summit ($2\frac{1}{2}$ h.). Slightly harder in reverse direction.

TORRE CASIANO DE PRADO   2622m.

102.   First of two summits on large rock spur projecting S from Te. del Llambrión. Most conveniently reached by ridge from Llambrión summit, down some short steep walls at first, II-. From Jermoso hut reverse approach path until S edge of the Llambrión hoyo can be crossed to foot of W face where a broken ledge line and short walls go up to summit, II ($1\frac{3}{4}$ h.). This peak has several important rock climbs, including the SE buttress, 300m., IV/V+, and E face, 300m., IV.

TORRE DE LAS MINAS DE CARBON   2595m.

103.   Outer summit formed on ridge of R. 102, most easily reached up broken W face, I+, $1\frac{3}{4}$ h. from Jermoso hut. Numerous climbs, sometimes on poor rock, include the W buttress, 300m., IV; S pillar, 300m., IV+; S face, 400m., V+; SE face, 300m., III+.

TORRE DE LAS LLASTRIAS   2598m.

104.   Fairly prominent hump on ridge running out NE from the Llambrión, reached in a few min. from col of same name, R. 21. Mapping hereabouts very bad.

TORRE DEL HOYO GRANDE   c. 2550m.

105.   Steep gable end of the Llastrias summit, a few short rock climbs.

EL PICION   2351m.

106.   Huge needle overlooking the Hoyo Grande; a projection at end of Llambrión NE ridge.   Seen sideways on (E or W faces) it reveals itself as a broad tower.

TORRE DE LA PALANCA   2614m.

107.   Elongated mtn. some distance along ridge extending NW from the Llambrión.   Most easily climbed from Jermoso hut by its SSW spur, I, 2 h.   The terraced NE face of 350m. has routes of V.

TORRE DIEGO MELLA   2484m.

108.   First tower formed on ridge extending generally SW from Te. de la Palanca, and enclosing N side of Llambrión hoyo behind Jermoso hut.   Several good short climbs.

TORRE DELGADO UBEDA   2473m.

109.   Coming down, second tower on ridge of R. 108.   Similar good short climbs.

TORRE DE PEÑALBA   2442m.

110.   Bold, attractive third (lowest) tower on ridge of R. 108. Popular rock climbing venue virtually justifying existence of Jermoso hut which is only 15 min. away from start of climbs. Rock generally excellent.   Normal route follows gullies cutting terraced walls forming W facet, 250m., III+.   A. Martinez, 8 August, 1944.   Among half a dozen good routes are: SW face, 250m., IV; S Face Dièdre, 300m., V-.

CABRALES CENTRAL AND WEST

PICO TESORERO   2570m.

Simple pyramid peak of modest aspect, strictly a mtn. walker's
summit.   Located at junction knot of ridges in physical centre
of the Central Massif, it is far and away the most instructive
and superior viewpoint in all the Picos.   Mandatory ascent for
all visitors with serious touring and exploratory intents, probably the second most frequented peak in the region after Vieja
while having rougher approach tracks.   Comfortable day outing
from head of cableway. Probably climbed by John Ormsby, 1871.

111.   <u>East-South-East Ridge</u>. Traditional normal route, upper
part of track badly eroded, steep and loose and better for descent, L. From cableway as for R. 1, 3 to below top of Rojos col
as described in R. 3, then by first variation towards ridge gap
behind shoulder/step above col ($2\frac{1}{4}$ h.).   About 25m. below gap
leave track, move L up a short narrow defile and exit L or R
round a large hole to small plateau with an upper col/gap at
same level on R.   Above, steep rock mounts towards Los
Urrieles (2501m.).   A vague, intermittent track winds up easy
rock steps on L side of latter, in a rising traverse for some
distance to a regular slope high above a large snow hollow. The
track improves, mounting gradually across S side of Los Urrieles, and is joined by another track coming from snow hollow
below.   Then it rises more steeply in loose reddish gravel to
join ESE ridge at a broad red saddle between Los Urrieles and
Tesorero.   Follow steepening ridge to a grey section.   Keep L
below this until a short gully cutting R for 15m. can be climbed
to crest again.   Follow near crest on track to better rock and
cairned summit. Some 50m. distance away over large blocks
is another summit of about the same height (45 min., 3 h. from
cableway).

Variation.   Just below red ridge saddle a little track traverses
L below the SE facet to join upper part of SE ridge - a better finish on continuous rocks, I+.

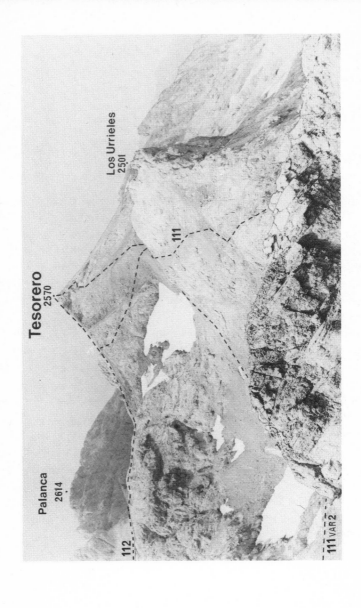

Variation. From Verónica biv. hut, as for R.18 to cross broad rock bridge dividing two small snowfields (15 min.). At far side turn R and descend blocks alongside snowfield for 100m. distance to turn by moving L (N) and well above its base a spur above which falls E. It is only possible to complete this turning movement at one pt. without encountering difficulties, across a broken band between slabs. It leads out to lower edge of the large snow hollow below summit pyramid. Cross snow or go over large blocks just below it, to join track on far side below S flank of Los Urrieles. Take steep zigzag track to junction noted above (1¼ h. from Verónica hut to summit).

112.   <u>South-East Ridge</u>. Superior route, good rock, I+. From Verónica hut, as for R.18 to cross broad rock bridge dividing two small snowfields (15 min.). At far side ascend steep scree diagonally L towards pt. where an intervening subsidiary spur above, running down E, abuts the buttressed end of SE ridge. Keep going up L towards a large terrace/ramp rising L below buttress, until a gully can be entered and climbed R, leading precisely to pt. where spur is joined to side of buttress. From little saddle so reached, climb steep flank of buttress/step on excellent rock, in grooved ribs with short slabby walls, trending R at first, then direct, and lastly somewhat L to top of buttress forming outer end of ridge (60m., I+). Follow wide horizontal ridge over a saddle and go up with increasing steepness to summit ridge. Climb this as directly as possible, minor turning movements on L side never more than 8m. from crest (bits of I+) to finish by a continuous scramble at summit cairn (1¼ h. from Verónica, 3¼ h. from cableway via Verónica).

COLLADA LABRADA   2410m.
113.   Between P. Tesorero and P. Arenizas, tedious trackless scree pass between Boches hoyo and Hoyo Grande.

PICO ARENIZAS N. 2515m. S. 2502m.

114. Multiple summits on main ridge with highest at N end. Can be reached from Boches hoyo by long rising traverse to gap between the two main summits, then a scramble to top, I. Or by NW ridge from Arenizas Baja pass, R. 18, 19, I+.

HORCADA ARENIZAS BAJA (or DE CAÍN) 2339m.

115. Between P. Arenizas and To. del Oso, important pass and access route, see R. 18, 19.

TIRO DEL OSO 2571m.

116. Prominent craggy eminence and ridge junction where the Pardida-Neverón and Cerredo wings go their separate ways. Long loose ramp on N side provides easiest route, I+.

HORCADA ARENIZAS ALTA (or DON CARLOS) 2410m.

117. Between To. del Oso and P. Boada, important pass and access route, see R. 18, 19.

PICO BOADA 2513m.

118. Secondary pt. above Arenizas Alta pass, by SW ridge from latter, II. Easier from small col on its NE side.

TORRE PARDIDA 2572m.

119. Tremendous viewpoint, otherwise of little interest, accessible by easy N slopes reached from R. 17.

NEVERÓN DE URRIELLO N. 2559m. S. 2548m.

120. El Neverón. Another outstanding viewpoint, more frequented than the Pardida, normally reached from R. 17 by the NW spur, I+.

HORCADA ARENERA DE ABAJO 2279m.

121. Between El Neverón and Neverón del Albo, important pass and access route, see R. 17.

NEVERÓN DEL ALBO 2430m.

122. First of three summits forming the Cuetos del Albo sub group. Complicated access from Ubeda hut side of R. 17.

PICO ALBO 2442m.

123.   Sunrise Peak.   A long W gully rises to NW ridge gap pt.
2394m.   This gully is reached from below W side of R. 17 by a
complicated traverse N, I+.

CUETO ALBO 2441m. (2414m.)

124.   Simple NW slope, tedious to reach.   Prime candidate
for the cableway threat.

TORRE DE COELLO 2584m.

125.   Giant flying buttress projecting SW from main ridge at
pt. 2518m. after To. del Oso.   This buttress overlooks upper
section of the Hoyo Grande and rises directly above R. 18.
Main ridge pt. can be reached by NE debris slope at head of
Cerredo hoyo, then a short linking crest to summit, I.   The
flying buttress has a very steep WSW face, 400m., V; and a
slabbier SE face, 300m., IV/V+.   Several possibilities for
new routes, not least evident the buttress crest.

COLLADO BERMEJA 2495m.

126.   Between Te. de Coello and Te. Bermeja, debris slopes
on NE side easily attained from Cerredo hoyo; on SW (Hoyo
Grande) side has two rockbands with traces of a path, II-.

TORRE BERMEJA 2606m.

127.   Because of proximity to the Cerredo, much frequented
as an additional summit when latter is climbed, and done thus
by Cerredo first ascensionists.   From highest terrace system
under E face of Cerredo, R. 128, traverse S usually with snow
patches under Bermeja-Cerredo gap 2590m. and ascend rough
slope at a moderate angle for 10 min.   Now ascend diagonally
R over a big ramp to summit on L, I- (30 min. from terrace).
Hoyo Grande side of this peak has several technical climbs.

TORRE CERREDO 2648m.

Lofty Tower.   As the highest mtn. in the Picos, naturally one
of the most frequented.   At the present time most ascents are
made from the Ubeda hut, but the new Cabrones hut offers a
short approach.   Long from the Verónica hut, and a marathon
expedition if done from the cableway without an overnight halt.
A bonus offered by the mtn. is the wide variety of climbs rising
through all grades of difficulty, with a splendid outlook amid

FROM SW

B

Cerredo
2648

A   C   E   F   G   H

D

K   J

FROM SW

A B   C   E F   Naranjo   H

D   G

J   K   L

grand and remote rock scenery. However, as a rock climbing venue not quite in the same class as the neighbouring P. de los Cabrones. An ice axe should be taken in any season. First ascent: Saint-Saud, P. Labrouche with F. Sallés, J. Suárez, 30 July, 1892.

128.   East Face Normal Route. After generally laborious approaches, a pleasant finish in a rather loose chimney at first then nice open staircase, I+. Reach Cerredo hoyo upper cwm bed from Ubeda hut by R. 17. Instead of descending R (NW), continue traversing SW to cross a slight saddle low down in NW ridge of Te. de la Pardida, beyond which a descending traverse leads over rubble into snowy cwm bed ($2\frac{1}{4}$ h.). From Cabrones hut by reversing R. 17 and following R side of Negro-Cerredo hoyo system into upper cwm (1 h.). From Verónica hut by R. 18 to edge of snowbed in Cerredo hoyo where, to save time, it is worth making a traverse above cwm bed over loose rubble slopes cut by short rockbands to approach mtn. ($3\frac{3}{4}$ h.).

Cerredo E

BERMEJA forepeak

127

128

129

RISCO SAINT–SAUD

128

From top of cwm bed ascend steep unpleasant slope on R side, under E flank of mtn. until you are below large snow patches in line with Bermeja-Cerredo gap. Now work R over scree and blocks and normally cross L end of large snow patch into a shallow scree gully in line with gap. Ascend loose gully and exit R to climb trending R over an area of honeycomb rock and terraces to finish on large upper terrace system with snow patches directly under E face. Go along to R end, under last gully cutting R side of face. Climb loose gravel (snow patch) into this gully which at first slants R towards the enclosing NE ridge at level of the big pinnacle named after Saint-Saud and marking base of latter ridge. 30m. up gully avoid a chockstone pitch by climbing vertical wall R on large holds to a ledge (8m., II-). Note, this can be avoided by taking R side of subsidiary rib bordering R side of gully to reach same ledge, shattered rock, 30m., I+. Enter a cave hollow in gully and exit L to open E face. Climb this trending L, getting further away from the gully all the time, boot marked and fairly obvious with short steep steps divided by little ledges, some loose rock, finally mounting to a projection L. Ascend this to main ridge in 15m. and summit on L (1-1$\frac{1}{4}$ h. from upper cwm bed).

129.　<u>North-East Ridge</u>. Foot of ridge (gap) is marked by the conspicuous horned Risco Saint-Saud, which can be climbed as a detour. First rate scramble, 80m., II+, very sustained, rock excellent. (Note, larger tower at bottom of this ridge is Te. Labrouche). From foot of E face gully snow patch, R. 128, climb shattered rock diagonally R to small scree shoulder then descend a similar distance under slabby wall to enter a chimney/gully. Descend a few m. then climb broken wall directly in 25m. to ridge gap (15 min.). Alternatively, from upper terraces below E face traverse horizontally R and downwards on rock and scree to a pt. in line with the Risco. Now ascend entire length of chimney/gully using pleasant rocks on L side.

Follow slabby crest with good holds to a step taken at L edge, exposed, then more slabs to a blunt crest with good holds L, finally a vertical step on small jugs to finish with scrambling to forepeak, then summit further L ($1\frac{1}{4}$ h. from foot of normal route gully).

Risco Saint-Saud. From pt. in chimney/gully 25m. below the ridge gap, climb broken wall trending R into an alcove. Move R to a rib and continue to sharp summit, II, sustained, 10 min. N side of this pinnacle gives longer, more difficult climbs.

130. East Face Direct. L of an obvious straight chimney/ gully cutting face, climb trending L to buttress outline, then by crest to top, III+/IV.

131. South Ridge. From Bermeja-Cerredo gap, short fierce climb on upper step, V.

132. North Face Routes. This side presents a slabby NE wall bordered L by the Risco Saint-Saud and NE ridge, and R by a prominent corner/ridge forming a N spur. To its R is a huge sub wall flanking an icy gully extending to a pinnacled gap (2500m.) in NNW ridge. The NE wall has a route starting on rib R of N spur and gully entrance, to cross L and reach obvious shoulder on spur rather more than 1/3rd distance up, then slanting L to finish up a groove parallel with NE ridge, 330m., IV (1978). N spur direct, from bottom mostly just L of its crest, 350m., V (1976). NE gully approach by broken ground on its R side, serious mixed climbing, 500m., III+/IV (1956). All these routes commence out of cwm at top of Jou Negro which has a 35-40° headwall, often snowy.

133. West-South-West Spur. Large projection falling to the lower Hoyo Grande, various routes of 300m., III to V-.

TORRE LABROUCHE 2510m.

134. Substantial tower at foot of Cerredo NE ridge. Its inner side gap is pt. 2400m. First recorded ascent, 1943. Numerous short technical climbs. Easiest way, from Cerredo hoyo up steep scree and rock into shallow gully on S side below gap, then more scree higher up. Take gully system in S facet, started below gap, to exit R near top with summit further R (III). By very steep corner ridge from gap itself, IV+.

PICO DE LOS CABRONES 2553m.

A connoisseur's peak, one of the most desirable summits in the
Picos, also one of the most difficult. Already with a goodly
number of excellent climbs, combined with proximity to the new
Cabrones hut, it is destined to become one of the foremost play-
grounds in region. The peak and its satellite pinnacles rise
from the back of the crater-like floor of the Cabrones hoyo on
N side, while the deep hollow of the Negro hoyo enhances the
SE side aspect. If approached by R. 17 from Ubeda hut, add
$1\frac{3}{4}$-$2\frac{1}{4}$ h. to all routes. Ice axe nearly always required. First
ascent: G. Schulze, 1906.

135. South Ridge. The usual route, however technically the
same standard as other ways. 350m., III. From Cabrones
hut contour round base of pt. 2314m. and go up and down over
slabby ribs to enter the Negro hollow. Follow bed (snow) to
below L side of SE face, on your R. A broken spur descends
from lower serrated step of S ridge. Go up steep scree/snow
and move L on to spur, following its crest line to where it
merges into side of step. On the R a staircase/ramp to a gully
(snow) giving access to S ridge at an obvious gap behind the step.
Follow this weakness (II+) to ridge. Now climb a short wall
(III) and continue on or near slabby crest to another short pitch
of III before reaching sharp summit ($2\frac{1}{4}$ h. from hut).

136. South-East Face Direct. A snowfield crosses face at mid
height. Start from lowest rock toe in summit line, very good
slab climb on nice rock, 425m., IV.

137. North-East Ridge. Rises from gap separating mtn. from
the 3 Ag. de los Cabrones. From Cabrones hut cross Cabrones
hoyo to scree slope (snow) under N face, and climb this labor-
iously between rockbands at top into gully below gap. The gully
has short chockstone pitches. From gap climb fine airy crest,
mostly slabby and sustained at II+ with short bits of III to the
summit ($1\frac{3}{4}$ h. from hut).

138. North Face Chimneys. In summit line, curve L and
back R, 300m., III+.

139. North-West Ridge. Schulze route, technically only II+
but rock rather poor though used as much as R. 135. At back
of Cabrones hoyo go up steep scree and rubble to foot of ridge
near saddle 2319m. Turn initial tower on L side and go up
first short gully beyond to crest. Follow staircase ridge with
several steep bits in a fine position, numerous large loose
flakes (2 h. from hut).

140.   <u>West Face</u>.   Above the Dobresengos ravine (R. 145), about 400m. high, no climbs traced but several obvious possibilities.

141.   <u>Cabrones-Cerredo Main Ridge Traverse</u>.   Noted as one of the finest ridge traverses in the Picos.   No personal information.   Delicate and exposed, pitches of IV, 800m. long.   1st traverse, A. & J. M. Régil, 1958.

AGUJAS DE LOS CABRONES   c. 2400m.

142.   A tight group of three towers forming lower extension to the Cabrones NE ridge.   Various routes on both flanks out of the Cabrones and Negro hoyos, 200m., III to V.

PICO DOBRESENGOS   2395m.

143.   Triple summit with N (2382m.) and S (2385m.) tops, and an outlying NW top (2390m.).   Rocky mtn. flanking W side of Cabrones hoyo.   Normal route by broken rock at R edge of E face, then ENE ridge, I+ ($1\frac{3}{4}$ h. from Cabrones hut).   E face R-hand route, III/III+.   Several other possibilities.

CUETOS DEL TRAVE   2241m.

144.   Various tower tops along ridge running towards the Amuesa pasture.   Technical climbs of 300m.

o   o   o

Jou Trasllambrión - Hoyo Grande - Dobresengos Ravine

145.   Long, deep gorge system extending at top from the Ca. Blanca (2310m., R. 18) down to head of the Cares gorge at Caín hamlet (513m.), over a ground distance of 8 km.   Its ascent / descent is quite complicated and must be rated I+.   Almost always done in descent, quite frequently.   A path line marked on most maps is inconsistent and often wrong.   There is no path in the top section, the best line in the middle section is not obvious, while the last 2 km. to Caín are quite easy to follow.

Coming down, as for R. 18, continue in bed through what is the outer part of the Hoyo Grande and go over a scree rim into the main double part of the hoyo under Te. Bermeja-Cerredo. Keep along the R side of this depression area, with short reascents, and pick up a track traversing in from same direction from above.   Continue down R side on debris to head of the Dobresengos ravine proper.   While there are tempting looking easy slopes on R side of ravine, start working across bed to descend L side.   Stay on this side to follow bits of track until you are directly under the Cabezas Altas (1878m.). Now keep straight down steep rough ground in zigzags to a pasture area (1540m.), then traverse slightly L along base of enclosing ridge and wind round a side ravine below the Co. de Pando to a saddle on ridge directly above Caín. Take track down W side to small road before bridge giving access to hamlet (3-3½ h. from the Ca. Blanca).

Cares Gorge

146.   Garganta Divina, showpiece gorge of the Picos, magnificent rock scenery, nearly 12 km. long on the ground between Caín and Puente Poncebos. In this downward direction, 3½ h. In ascent, 5 h. While the vertical interval is only 300m. there is another 150m. of reascent and descents. Exposed and care required in many places, grade L The route is fairly obvious except for the start in ascent. Jeep road now goes some distance past the Jaya bridge fork L for Bulnes, although in a short way it has been blocked by boulders to prevent motorists going further.   The first small gravel track in yellow stone on the R after Jaya bridge must be taken (after a similar one marked "Camarmeña"), and not the better looking horizontal trail near bed which eventually drops to the river.

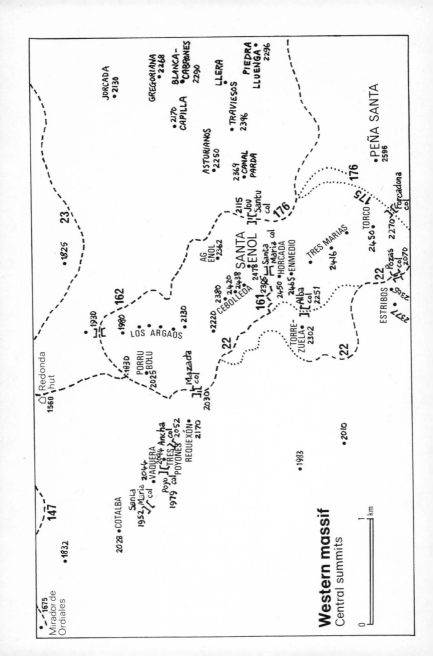

Western massif
Central summits

WESTERN (CORNIÓN) MASSIF

MAIN RIDGE NORTH-WEST WING

MIRADOR DE ORDIALES 1691m. 1675m.

147.   All paths near to or leading away from the Redonda hut
are marked with poor precision on maps. This viewpoint is a
tourist excursion par excellence, and the main path to it forks
R from R. 15 some 10 min. before hut, crossing the Jungumia
valley lower down. From hut descend L side of valley for 5
min. to pick up aforesaid waymarked trail. This makes a rising traverse over valley flank and returns L to cross a saddle;
then traversing W again it crosses another saddle to enter a
grassy/hollow area, at the far side of which is the tomb and
slab inscription of Pedro Pidal, founder of the Picos National
Park, and a sheer escarpment edge beside a hillock (1691m.)
overlooking the Dobra valley nearly 1000m. below, I-, 1 h.

PICO COTALBA 2028m.

148.   From Ordiales (R. 147) follow main ridge SE over grass,
a few rocks, lastly rubble and blocks to this excellent viewpoint
commanding NW side of Cornión massif, I- (40 min. from the
Mirador, about $1\frac{3}{4}$ h. from Redonda hut). From Ca. de Santa
Maria (1952m.) on far side of summit dome an interesting descent can be made due N between the Huerta and Juñazu hoyos
back to first saddle on R. 147.

TIRO DE LA CANAL VAQUERA 2044m.

149.   Shapely conical peak on main ridge after Cotalba, usually
climbed (I) as part of the complete traverse from Ordiales to
Mazada, R. 157.

TORRE DE LOS TRES POYONES 2094m.

150.   Three large tower summits, the highest on main ridge
before El Requexón, extending N from main ridge and separated
from the Vaquera (R. 149) by Ha. del Poyo or Pollo (1979m.).
Towers are numbered from highest, 3, 2, 1. Main ridge traverse of 3rd (highest) tower, I+. Outstanding training ground
for local climbers, rock nearly always perfect. Numerous fine
climbs, 100m. to 250m. in most grades of difficulty. The E side
above Requexón hoyo is reached from Redonda hut in 1 h. by
moving R out of grassy trench under Porru Bolu on R. 22, and
traversing W and N into big hollow beyond. The W side can be
reached as for E by crossing below foot of last (1st) tower with

PORRU BOLU
NE SIDE

gully

EL REQUEXÓN
E RIDGE

155

154

152

POYONES
2094

one section of steep slabs. Or from 1st saddle on R. 147, by ascent route towards Ca. de Santa Maria (R. 148), traces of a path, and near foot of last slope working L into the Vaquera ravine which runs up below W side of towers, 1 h. None of these towers can be climbed by their faces or internal ridges below III+. Traverse of all three by linking ridges, IV+. New route possibilities.

HORCADA ANCHA   2052m.

151.   Wide debris saddle in main ridge between Poyones main tower (2094m.) and El Requexón, an access corridor used on N side, or crossed when moving between latter two summits. On N side, coming out of the Requexón hoyo, ascend towards L side steep broken slabby grooves, scree and blocks, I.

EL REQUEXÓN   2170m.

Important secondary peak on main ridge, of dome shaped profile, like the Poyones noted for good rock, and a worthy objective for training.

152.   <u>East Ridge</u>. Normal route, I. From Redonda hut reach Mazada col by R. 22. Cross slabby ground E and descend to a lower col in a few min. Either climb a broken rock rib in main ridge line or turn it R in a little ravine, and go up stony ground, over a rockhead, across a slight dip and finally along crest of scree mound to foot of final rib. Step down L and climb steep broken slabby rock L of crest line for 25m. to rubble and blocks leading to broad summit ($1\frac{3}{4}$ h. from Redonda hut).

153.   <u>West Ridge Flank</u>. A classic scramble on firm rock, invariably used to traverse mtn., II, sustained. From Redonda hut go into Requexón hoyo as advised in R. 150, and exit from rear by R. 151 to Ha. Ancha. Go up to foot of first ridge step then make a rising traverse R over steep broken rock to enter a gully. Climb this with pleasant little pitches to summit ridge and top 50m. further along ($2\frac{1}{4}$ h. from Redonda hut).

154.   <u>South-East Face Gullies</u>. Two parallel gullies close together, easily reached from R. 152 final approach. About 200m., IV for either. Plenty of unclimbed rock hereabouts.

LOS ARGAOS E side 159

2064

saddle
1930

155.   <u>North Face</u>.   Direct route, 200m., V. R-hand, IV.

COLLADO DE LA MAZADA   2030m.

156.   Also called Ha. de Cebolleda, one of the most important ridge crossings in the Western Massif, primarily giving access to W side of main ridge, see R. 22.

157.   <u>Ordiales - Mazada Main Ridge Traverse</u>.   First class scramble over all summits and cols mentioned under R. 147, 148, 149, 150, 151, 153, 152, in this order, highly recommended, 6 h. round trip from Redonda hut, II.

PORRU BOLU   2025m.

158.   Huge pillar with serrated top, detached from mtn. side (steep wall) on a minor ridge above R. 22, about 45 min. from Redonda hut.   Rock variable.   Its frontal N face above path is enormously impressive and rises for 120m. giving a route of V+, A2.   NE face has a meandering route of V, and a more sustained one of same standard further L.   Routes on W face are at least V+, A1/2.   Other possibilities.   Normal route takes NE gully between pillar and main wall, and from separation gap ascends rear side of pillar by slanting line, III+.   First ascent, 1934.

LOS ARGAOS   2064m.

159.   Side ridge of 5 tower/pinnacles and other minor teeth extending N from outer shoulder of Tes. de Cebolleda, treated as a simple and convenient rock practice ground.   First tower is directly above first mini saddle (1930m.) on R. 162, 45 min. from Redonda hut.   Main ridge traverse, grassy in places, using all possible dodges, II+, but normally taken on or near crest at III-.   Nice little slab routes of III on E side of towers. The steeper wall and groove aspect of higher W (hut) side gives routes of 175m., IV and V, and several artificial climbs.   Maps disagree about height of these towers, probably having copied each other with simple transposition of last two figures, but this is rather academic.

TORRES DE CEBOLLEDA   2438m.

160.   Complicated craggy preamble to the little Peña Santa, three measured tower summits and a big cliff aspect on SW side.   Climbed quite frequently with most interest in continuing to the parent peak.   On SW side (R. 22) its smooth striated walls dominate this part of main ridge and obscure the Peña Santa de Enol.   The relative positions of the two summit groups is more

easily appreciated from NE side (R. 162). Normal route by traversing NW ridge over tower 1 (2380m.) and tower 2 (2420m.) offers pitches of II+ to last gap before tower 3 (2438m.). The final ridge goes at IV- and III. Route is started 5 min. over the Mazada col, R. 22, by ascending grass and scree into obvious opening below main ridge and tower 1 (3-3½ h. from Redonda hut). Several quality routes out of same opening to tower 2, and on S wall further round to R, 250-300m., IV and V. Further R still on this side the big wall below tower 3, out of couloir of R. 161, appears to be unclimbed.

Continuation of main ridge traverse to the little Peña Santa involves climbing or turning the small pyramid Ag. de Gua standing above the Cebolleda-Peña Santa de Enol gap (III+) and then taking R side of final buttress/ridge (IV).

PEÑA SANTA DE ENOL   2478m.

Widely known as: Torre de Santa Maria. Colloquially: Little Peña Santa - to distinguish it from its mighty neighbour across the Jou Santu - the Big Peña Santa (de Castilla). Not an objective for walkers, this major peak presents quite hazardous ground and demands mountaineering experience. By following path R. 162 along N base all main features can be readily identified. The summit area is invisible from all points along R. 22, 161 on SW/S side, but this is the more popular approach. The N side is cut by a V-wedge cwm dividing our peak from the Cebolleda, and this is filled with a permanent, steep snowfield, the Cemba Vieya (=cold snow). Access to all routes on S side is by the Ha. de Santa Maria, a col in main ridge dividing mtn. from Te. de la Horcada-Enmedio group. This zone is badly depicted on some maps, also with tracks shown crossing wrong part of main ridge, inviting the inexperienced into dangerous situations. First ascent (by Grieta Rubia): Saint-Saud, P. Labrouche and party, 19 September, 1891.

161.   <u>South Side Normal Route</u>. Final part takes huge gully/ ramp, now exceedingly loose, called Grieta Rubia (Red Crack), invisible until you are below it. Short technical pitches of II.

From Redonda hut follow R. 22 over the Mazada col to zigzags under a wide scree opening so noted. Track continues up this big gully slope and peters out 80m. below conspicuous col at the top. Ascend finely balanced scree and blocks, best on L side but hard work everywhere, to Ha. de Santa Maria (2305m.), 2¼ h. On the other (E) side make a slightly descending traverse L, facing out, for 150m. distance, height loss 35m., over broad

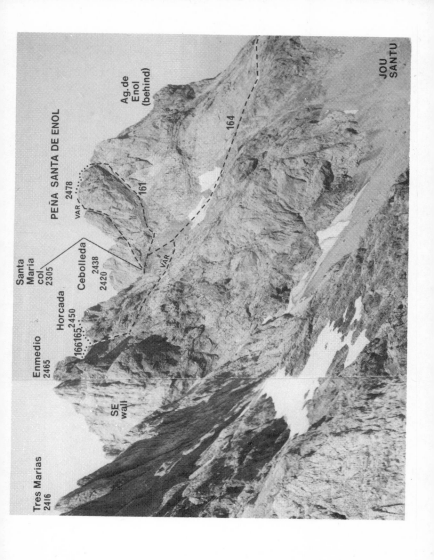

Tres Marias
2416

Enmedio
2465

166 165

Horcada
2450

Santa
Maria
col
2305

Cebolleda
2438
2420

PEÑA SANTA DE ENOL

VAR
2478

161

VAR

Ag. de
Enol
(behind)

164

SE
wall

JOU
SANTU

headslope of E side gully, following fringe of steep rock along to a vertical rockband closing bottom of a large ramp area seen partly above. Step on to wall and toe traverse R to narrow crack near R end. Climb this direct (10m., II, sustained) into an open groove and continue (12m., I+) to delicate landing on ramp. Go up broad ramp in loose zigzags, working L into red gully corner which is taken for 10m. (I+) before breaking R again. Ramp steepens into low terraced walls of better rock. Go up centre, trending L to base of smooth walls. From last ledge make a toe traverse horizontally L across top of slab with pushout wall above, delicate; or hand traverse at the toe level with small footholds on slab (either way exposed, 6m., II); now move up L for 5m. round a shattered pulpit, then pull up to stance at top (II). Follow broken rock trending L into upper gully bed which is climbed for a few m. to ridge gap at top of the Grieta Rubia. On the other side is the N side ramp. Go down this for 30m. to first big open corner on L. Climb R side of corner, trending R up grassy rock to continuous short steps (I+), emerging at notch in summit ridge only a few m. from top on R (45 min., 3 h. from Redonda hut).

Direct Variation. This is really unconnected with the normal route and allows climbers to reach the summit by climbing straight up from the Santa Maria col. All the route can be seen and looks deceptively easy, but is not. 150m., III+. From col go straight up broken rock for a few m. then make a rising traverse R over flake slabs to enter a gully/groove slanting R to L (II). Take gully direct with short chimney pitches and walls of III/III+ and an awkward wall at L near ridge at top and just W of summit.

162. North Side Ramp Normal Route. Less frequented because of the Cemba Vieya, which is often ice, but climbers will find it more varied than the Grieta Rubia, though possibly less interesting. Ice axe essential, crampons useful, II. The two routes afford a splendid simple traverse of mtn.

From Redonda hut ascend grass to rear to join and follow main path up R side of valley, eventually reaching a fork at top

of a grass slope called Llampa Cimera (1830m.), 30 min. The
L branch is taken into a boulder hollow. Go up this in graded
zags to a small grass saddle (1930m.) below last tower of Los
Argaos (15 min.). The excellent path now traverses SE above
a hoyo system, later descending and reascending with twisty
sections till you reach at a comparatively high pt. again a grassy
slope rising towards mtn. Further along grass gives way to a
large bank of slabs. Turn off R before latter (20 min.) and go
up earthy slope trending L to rock maze at top. Work R or L
round a mini hoyo to reach and cross scree, blocks and snow
patches below the big snowfield wedge. Climb to wedge by steep
loose blocks and broken slabs at L side, fairly close to sheer
wall of Ag. de Enol further L. So reach foot of snowfield (35 min.).
Climb this near L side with increasing steepness, but not long,
40° at top, bergschrund or roture possible. Step off snow/ice
awkwardly onto steep rock and follow a ledge line L (I+) to a
broken wall area below a big regular scree ramp rising R to L.
Climb either of two vague chimney/groove lines in this short
wall (15m., II-) and go up long ramp easily to last big corner
opening on R before ridge gap at top, where R. 161 is joined
(50 min., $2\frac{1}{2}$ h. from Redonda hut).

163. North Spur and Aguja de Enol (2362m.)

This spur provides all the worthwhile technical climbing on the
little Peña Santa, and it terminates abruptly with the prominent
Enol tower. Several routes on the Cemba Vieya wall up to N
spur crest behind tower, generally IV on good rock, while crest
itself is II+; the other flank is loose. Climbs on the Aguja are
more specialised and all the N spur from this pt. is III-. Reach
N foot of the Aguja as for R. 162, moving L below last steep
debris slope before snowfield ($1\frac{1}{2}$ h. from hut). Sloping scree
terraces. For normal route, descend L round base into shallow
opening on E side with steep buttress/step further L. Climb
slabby gully opening to ridge gap and tower top, pitches of III.
N face: several routes of 200m., IV to V, converge at 2/3rds
height to make a common finish L under triangular summit wall
and exposed exit wall L (IV).

HORCADA DE SANTA MARIA   2305m.

164.   Between Peña Santa de Enol and Te. de la Horcada, this col is cited in Spanish publications as a touring route, but we do not recommend it as such, except for climbers. W side is described under R. 161, I-. The E side gully falls 200m. to vicinity of Boca del Jou Santu (R. 176) at N edge of this famous hoyo. Steeper and looser than W side, and has a large snow-field groove in middle section, axe necessary, I/I+. It is important to note that very steep bottom section is avoided alt-ogether by a slabby ramp on N side which runs down conveniently to the Boca, 30 min. in descent, 1 h. in ascent.

TORRE DE LA HORCADA   2450m.

165.   Some maps, 2456m. A most recommendable viewpoint. Several good routes, III to V with potential for more, on W ridge and its two flanks above R. 161 approach to Santa Maria col. Normal route, with a lot of loose rubble, takes obvious scree ramp from foot of W ridge (snowpatch), a few m. from R. 161 zigzags into Santa Maria W gully. Go up ramp at 35° to constriction with blocks and exit trending L into small scree hollow rising to saddle in main ridge between this peak and the Enmedio. Climb ridge on L, keeping slightly L of crest ($2\frac{1}{2}$ h. from Redonda hut). Note: Ridge from Santa Maria col is cut off at 1/3rd height by a large gash (abseil).

TORRE DE ENMEDIO   2465m.

166.   Turreted peak rising directly above Jou Santu which en-hances its height. Normal route as for R. 165 to saddle then up R side of main ridge on R to middle of 3 small towers, I+ ($2\frac{1}{2}$ h. from Redonda hut). Also possible from Santa Maria col by descending E side gully for 50m. until a gully/ramp weakness on R can be entered and climbed by a steep rising traverse under Te. de la Horcada to dividing saddle (II-). Technical routes on SE wall.

TORREZUELA   2302m.

167.   Attractive mtn. crowning side ridge and divided from the Enmedio by the broad Alba col, R. 22. By sharp, exposed W ridge from this col, II-, recommended, 20 min. Various gully and wall routes to R on N wall of mtn.

TORRE DE LAS TRES MARIAS   2416m.

168.   Not named on most maps. Deep gap (2272m.) in main ridge separates this peak from Enmedio. Rarely climbed, awkward of access, II. Some maps show dotted line track over gap; this must be fiction, probably very loose and grade II.

EL TORCO E

PORRO

169

JOU SANTU

TORRE DEL TORCO   2450m.

El Torco. Regular, smooth, slabby, bulbous towers above the
Jou Santu, marking end of main ridge NW wing above La Forcadona. Good rock, more interesting than any summit leading
back to the little Peña Santa. Sensational view of big Peña Santa.

169. <u>East Face Gully</u>. First rate mountaineering route with
a minimum of loose terrain, mixed climbing, axe necessary,
300m., II+. As for R.162,176 to saddle under rock hillock pt.
2027m. It is quicker not to go over latter. Bear R towards
inner end of Jou Santu with a rough descending traverse SSW to
rock crater forming its rear below the Forcadona snowfield.
Climb honeycomb slabs and terraces in zags to rim of Jou, no
track, a few cairns. Now move R and ascend a narrow snow

wedge in main tower line, trending R with optional rocks on R
to an upper snow tongue joining main snowband running R below
E wall. Cross snowband R then L into 40° snowbed gully entrance
between main tower L and Porro del Torco tower R. Climb gully
above snow on sound rock with short chockstone pitches (II+) to
main ridge gap. Follow crest for 15m., then take a weakness
rising L over rough slabs (one bit III-) leading into an open gully.
Take this to a shoulder than climb last rocks on R to summit
($3\frac{3}{4}$ h. from Redonda hut)

170. East Face Direct. Several routes possible L of R. 169
gully, minimum IV. Others on slabby wall R, above terrace
snowband, along to fall line of rounded summit 2410m., all high
class technical climbing, about 220m.

171. West-North-West Face. An important climb of V/V+ takes
L side of this wall for 300m., reached from R. 22 in 20 min. from
near the Pozas col. Also possible to scale this side at III.

LOS ESTRIBOS 2305m.

172. First summit on important secondary ridge running WSW
from the Pozas col, R. 22. Normal route out of Pozas hoyo by
rockbands, scree ramps, etc. into gully leading to gap between
peak L and Te. de la Cabra Blanca R., then up short W ridge,
I+. E ridge from Pozas col, quite fine, III.

TORRE DE LA CABRA BLANCA 2377m.

173. As for R. 172 to foot of gully where a long ramp rises R to
W ridge which is followed to top, II. Several harder routes.

EL DIENTE 2355m.
GARITA CIMERA 2325m.

174. Heights suspect. Rock peaks most easily approached
from the Huerta hut.

LA FORCADONA 2270m.

175. Wide opening between El Torco and big Peña Santa, perhaps the only genuine "glacier" pass in the Picos, for all that
quite easy but rarely crossed except as an access route, I. NE
side approach as for R. 169 and continue in bed to large snowfield running up at a moderate angle to short gully and nick at
top (3-3$\frac{1}{2}$ h. from Redonda hut). SW side, steep and rough, down
to La Llerona on R. 22, not far from Huerta hut.

MAIN RIDGE EAST WING AND NORTHERN OUTLIERS

PEÑA SANTA DE CASTILLA   2596m.

Colloquially: Big Peña Santa. This great mtn. constitutes the whole of the short main ridge east wing. The northern outliers really belong to a ridge system running SW-NE from nearer the little Peña Santa.

Magnificent rock peak of classical form, by general consent the finest in the Picos. It consists of a single serrated E-W ridge above steep N and S walls. The ridge outer ends are studded with satellite towers that count as separate climbing areas. While the N side nowhere exceeds 350m. and is lapped by a long ragged snowfield, steep in parts, behind the Jou Santu, the S side rises to 550m. in an unbroken rock wall one km. wide above the Vega Huerta and ranks among the first 2 or 3 most important climbing areas in the Picos. From the summit, intriguing and curiously unsatisfactory distant panorama of the Central Massif looking like a prickly mattress emphasises isolation of the mtn. The easiest route having a short stiff entry pitch ensures that this mtn. remains the preserve of climbers.

First ascent: P. Labrouche with V. Marcos, F. Bernat-Sallés, 4 August, 1892. 2nd ascent: Pidal, Pérez, 1904. 3rd: Saint-Saud, Pérez, 1906. Probably not climbed by a British party until 1950.

176. North-West Face Narrow Gully. Except in favourable lighting conditions, barely visible to examination from a distance, located towards R side below second V gap in main ridge beyond and W of last summit ridge steps. Superb mountaineering route, one of the best of its class in the region. Rock good but loose stones between all gully pitches, II/II+ with a key entry pitch of III+, 350m. Waymarked at frequent intervals with yellow paint blobs. First ascensionists.

From Redonda hut, as for R. 162 and remain on good footpath now rising a little below Ag. de Enol (R. 163), passing small deep hole on L (fountain) and always SE to enter the Asturianos hoyo. Descend zags on L side and reascend far side to wide saddle, Boca del Jou Santu (c. 2115m., marked on maps variously, 2090, 2176). Magnificent, memorable prospect across wild Jou Santu ahead to Peña Santa filling background ($1\frac{3}{4}$ h.). Path now reduced to small track, goes off round L side of Jou Santu, a little downwards then rising similarly to reach broad saddle/corner under big rock hillock 2027m., though probably 2190m. (20 min.), below mtn. Here the main valley system bends L (E) as the Canal Parda upper cwm. The Balas fountain is some distance L and higher.

It is best to traverse hillock. Directly above saddle climb steepening rocks somewhat R and turn top R along slabs (I) to cross a honeycomb dip. Continue by easy slabs trending R, with a few cairns, to a short descent R into a narrow ravine. Follow its boulder bed (snow) to scree slope on L in summit fall line. Trend R up debris forming other side of gutter and mount a vague rib along top of rockband above the Forcadona snowfield, pursuant direction always SW and rising. Keep going steeply on shattered rock adjoining scree/snow band on L below NW face rocks, to reach a corner where a broad mass of rocks extends from main face down to snowfield and cuts off this approach. A few m. up to L is a narrow gully opening with continuation mostly invisible. The climb starts here, 45 min., $2\frac{3}{4}$-3 h. from Redonda hut.

Take grooved rocks with perfect holds on R side of narrow gully for 50m., until gully becomes more evident and open. At this pt. a deep branch has come up from R. Go up gully in short steps for a further 30m. to a big wall and chimney/crack pitch blocking further progress. All this section, I/I+; the big pitch looks at least IV+. Turn pitch by a narrow ramp L, returning R (20m., I+) into large hidden alcove stance. At the back climb a short undercut crack with awkward finish (7m., III+) to traverse a few m. R (I+) into bed above wall pitch. Abseil peg in place. Climb bed to a series of nice chimney/chockstone pitches, about 5, quite varied in technique and straightforward, mostly II, one II+, to loose exit slope with zags and broken rock leading to main ridge gap. In summit direction (E) is an initial tower. From gap traverse slabs horizontally on R (S) side (I+), or descend a little and traverse at lower level (I) into a gully

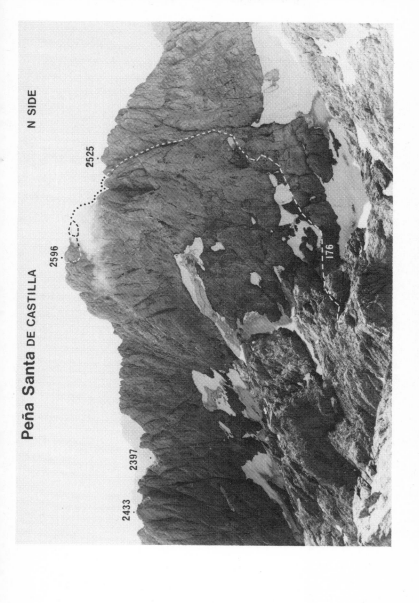

Peña Santa DE CASTILLA

N SIDE

2525

2596

2397

2433

176

beyond and below next ridge gap. Step across gully and climb opposite steep wall on excellent holds, trending L to top of next ridge step (30m., II). Trend R of ridge line and go up to a crack in slabby wall on this side. Climb this to top of next ridge step (25m., II+). Over the top is a tiny gap in crest. The normal way now descends L (N) side and in a few m. traverses L and slightly downwards over a slab band to a horizontal crevice (35m., II). To cross an intervening crevice/chimney, ascend slab above for 4m. (III, delicate), then move L for a few m.(III) across chimney where it has become a shallow gully below a ridge gap not far above. An easier and better way is to stay on main ridge, nicely exposed, and go into next gap below a vertical wall step. Descend gully on L (N) side to same pt. (II-). Both ways confusingly paint marked. Now continue traversing movement below main ridge on **N** side, generally slightly downwards with short reascents all across slabs, and after 50m. distance reach a steep rib flank. Climb this (8m., II), cross a platform shoulder and move round L into a narrow gully. You have now passed below summit line. Climb gully direct with L or R options at a steep pitch (10m., II+) to main ridge gap. Follow ridge on R for a few m. to summit enclosure wall (1 h. or less from start as noted, $3\frac{3}{4}$-4 h. from Redonda hut). Times based on roping up only for III+ pitch. In descent, a slither down a double rope is adequate for this, all other pitches being easier in reverse.

R. 176 notes. There is no comparable normal route on the S (Huerta hut) side. To reach R. 176 from S the best approach is over Forcadona pass (R. 22, 175), with a short rough scramble from snowfield to foot of gully, 2 h. from hut.

177. North-West Face Wide Gully. Situated about 150m. L of Narrow Gully, you pass below entrance on R. 176 final approach just after emerging from small ravine. It is best to enter gully higher up by following a broad slabby rib before latter ravine. At head of rib a ramp R enters gully at a triangular scree/snow patch. A little further up is a key wall pitch of IV, often reduced to III+ by a staircase of pegs in place. Above that the gully is easier than comparable section of R. 176, joining ridge

at next gap after latter's. Fairly frequented, considered quicker than R. 176 but less interesting.

178. <u>Other North Face Routes</u>. These are numerous. The chief ones, working L, and most of them involving crossing or ascending the steep dia gonal snowfield ramp: Wide Gully Left Ridge, 350m., IV+. North Face Buttonhole/Recess Zigzags, 300m., III+. North Face Direct, 300m., IV/IV+. North Spur (Direct and Indirect Finishes), 500m., min. IV+, max. V. North-East Face, 450m., III+ or harder.

179. <u>East-West Main Ridge Traverse</u>. One of most ambitious undertakings in the Picos, especially if attempted end to end, going over the Basares towers (2433m.) and finishing at Ag. del Corpus Christi. In this way, IV+, first accomplished over two days in 1974. More usual, much shorter and quite popular version first done in 1936 entails climbing S side by the main S wall ramp slanting R which starts R of summit line zone and leads to the double Brecha de los Cazadores (2385-2397m.) in E ridge, then along ridge with big initial step, a level section of small teeth and a final staircase section to summit, pitches of III and IV. Descent on S side is problematical and it is best to follow W ridge down to La Forcadona. The middle part (2525m.) entails numerous turning movements round steep tower steps, pitches of III+ (8 h.).

180. <u>South Face</u>. This tremendous wall offers a galaxy of first rate technical routes. A number of them give 600m. or more of high grade climbing. Among these are: Original Route Direct, IV+ (1947). Original Route, IV (1944). Pajaro Negro Gully, VI (1958). There is a huge unclimbed upper wall area between the last two routes. Shorter routes continue to R and L of this central zone. Approach from Vega Huerta hut is a simple downward walk with a track in grass and stones of 20 min. Possible ways up at L side of wall by ramp and chimney lines slanting R with pitches of III+ to reach R. 176 ridge gap.

AGUJA DEL GATO
AGUJA DEL CORPUS CHRISTI

181. Big rock prongs at end of SW branch ridge coming from Peña Santa W ridge, immediately above Vega Huerta. Both are covered with routes of c. 150m., especially Corpus Christi; the easiest ways are II+ and IV- respectively (1952).

TORRE DE LA CANAL PARDA 2369m.

182. Superior viewpoint, recommended. From Boca del Jou Santu (R. 176) go up steep blunt W ridge, turning rock bluffs and slabs L and R at will to summit, 45 min., I.

TORRE DE LOS TRAVIESOS   2396m.

183.   Normally reached by traversing W-E ridge from R.182 over saddle 2283m., 40 min., I.

TORRE BLANCA   2290m.

184.   Also known as Te. de los Cabrones. Complicated approach from R.176 track, quitted at N rim of Asturianos hoyo, working ENE up and down along N side of Parda-Traviesos group into big hoyo system rising S with easy but rough slopes to peak on L, I($1\frac{3}{4}$ h. from track).

PUNTA GREGORIANA   2268m.

185.   Named after Pérez. N end bastion of Te. Blanca sub group. Several rock climbs, normal route from the Jocada Blanca and NW ridge, I+.

TORRE DE PIEDRA LLUENGA   2296m.

186.   Double summit E-W on N side of Canal Parda upper cwm at its exit called El Boquete. Good climbing with no worthwhile route less than II/II+. The Jou Tras Piedra Lluenga is a wild deep hoyo on NE side.

TORRE ROBLIZA   2248m.
PEÑA BLANCA   2185m.

187.   Summits/heights transposed on some maps, with highest (SW end) also called Cabeza Llambreras. Notable rock peaks, best approach from Villaviciosa/Ario hut SW across Boca del Jaón (1910m.), track. Numerous short climbs.

LA VERDILLUENGA   2129m.

188.   Sharp peak above Boca del Jaón, I+.

CUVICENTE   2015m.
JULTAYO   1935m.

189.   Outstanding viewpoints above Cares Gorge, easily reached from Villaviciosa/Ario hut, I.

Classic Traverse. Jultayo, Verdilluenga, Te. Blanca, Los Traviesos, Te. de la Canal Parda; there are intermediate summits in same ridge line. This traverse is much praised in some Spanish publications, described as aerial but easy with a time of 4 h. In fact, to undertake it at grade II involves turning several sections of the main ridge, in and out of and up and down various hoyos (the ground is most contorted), and doubling back to bag all summits. Adhering to the ridge line throughout is probably III/III+, time nearer 7 h. from Ario hut to Boca del Jou Santu.

SOUTHERN OUTLIERS

This zone in a characteristic lunar landscape, but grassy and partly wooded all round its far flung lower slopes, comprises a forest of rock spires sprouting from ridges radiating like the spokes of a wheel from the centrally positioned highest summit, Te. Bermeja (2393m.). Vertical intervals out of the Valdeón on the S and E sides are considerable and tiring though with good tracks for much of the height. The Vega Huerta hut on N side is only in a good position for a limited number of peaks. Little visited at present, this zone has recently attracted new developments in rock climbing, notably on the Te. Ciega (2261m.) and Tes. de Aristas (2136m.); these pinnacles present a SE rock aspect of 500m. directly above Posada/Cordiñañes.

TORRE BERMEJA   2393m.

Vermilion Tower. Fairly common name in the Picos, climbed by Saint-Saud party in 1891 but had been ascended several times previously by local hunters.

190. <u>From Valdeón</u>. Classic way, though better for descent, I-/L. Leave Posada de Valdeón by lane on R, SW of village square, and cross Cares river to old unmade road on other (NW) side. Turn R and go along 200m. to a path forking L, uphill. Follow this quite steeply on a wooded rib until a junction is reached after 1¼ h., below first big rock barrier extending across this approach. Main path goes R (N). Keep L and follow numerous zigzags to an open rock slope funnelling up NW to a ravine opening in a barrier, towards its narrower, broken L side. Ascend this with path mostly gone to emerge in a hollow slanting L, called the Sedo del Gato. Follow this towards SSE ridge of mtn. ahead and close to pt. 2025m. bear R below ridge over rock hillocks and debris into a big gully cutting the next rock barrier extending R from the ridge. Ascend gully, called

Canal de Bufón, and so reach moderate slopes still on R side of aforesaid ridge. Continue up these slopes bearing L towards top of ridge and summit ($4\frac{3}{4}$ h.).

191. <u>From Panderruedas col or Huerta hut</u>. Much longer from former but with only a day sack quite pleasant, L From col, as for R. 13 to the Burro col under the Pico del Verde. Leave path and traverse NE and E just inside hillock 2172m. to enter hoyo under NNW face of Te. Bermeja, which is cut by several scree and block filled gullies. Almost any of these can be climbed with rough scrambling directly to summit ($4\frac{1}{2}$ h.). From Huerta hut reverse R. 13 to traverse off from same pt. ($2\frac{1}{4}$ h.). Also possible to start from Vegabaño hut, approaching by R. 14 to same pt. ($3\frac{3}{4}$ h.).

ADDENDA

Maps Numerous new maps have appeared since 1984 and others have gone permanently. Sheets of 1/25,000, usually of the pirate variety but of a good cartographical standard, are often available, and a superior overall area sheet of 1/50,000 (compared with the now withdrawn FEM map) was still available in 1990 – all from West Col Productions.

Caving and horse riding Both activities have grown appreciably in the late 1980s. Specialist information is available from West Col.

Brown bear pages 16,17. While thought to be extinct, a U.S.A research project over 2 years recently has established that bears have survived. Seven animals have been identified and monitored in the Valdeón area. Their exact location and movements are kept a closely guarded secret – especially from the gun-slinging local population.

Riaño page 38. Site and inhabitants removed in conjunction with huge dam project to harness the Elsa river. All roads hereabouts (parador closed permanently) realigned – see current T-21 Firestone map. Much trouble since 1986 over this project among the local people – including arson and shooting incidents.

Vega Redonda hut page 52. Burnt down and due to be rebuilt. Inquire at Covadonga.

Sotres village

INDEX

142